Redirected
"The Path that Led to Peace"

Aishia McQuillan

Aishia McQuillan

Rackhouse Publishing

Read to Learn, Write to Remember.

Copyright © Aishia McQuillan
All rights reserved. No part of this manuscript may be reproduced, stored in a retrieval system or transmitted in any form, or by any means, electronic, mechanical, photocopying, recording or otherwise, without prior permission of the author.

ISBN-13: 978-1-7371987-8-9

For information about custom editions, special sales, premium and bulk purchases, please contact:
Rackhouse Publishing Inc.
904-530-6754
rackhousepublishing.com

First Edition
Printed in the U.S.A

DEDICATION

This book is dedicated to all eight of my children, in order by age, LaDedrick Little, Tikeya James, Tyra McQuillan, Dasjuan Williams, Israel Carter, Jabari Jones, Tiana Mcquillan, and Tyrone McQuillan Jr. I thank you all for loving me and supporting me the way that you do. Each of you hold a special place in my heart and I love you all dearly.

To my grandbabies, Yesenia Williams & Jerome James III, G-Ma and Papa Tye love you always!

To Tyrone McQuillan, the amazing, incredible, irreplaceable, love of my life, I will never understand how I got to be so lucky to have someone like to be my forever mate. Since I know God makes no mistakes, I'd rather focus more on enjoying this beautiful bliss He put together. You have unselfishly supported me in all of my endeavors and sacrificed so much. I am forever grateful for you. That's why I dedicate this book to you as well, my love. Thank you for all you do. It does not go unnoticed. I love you endlessly.

CONTENTS

CHAPTER 1
THE BEGINNING (1)

CHAPTER 2
CHOICES & CONSEQUENCES (49)

CHAPTER 3
THE WRONG HANDS (85)

CHAPTER 4
THE RIGHT HANDS (111)

CHAPTER 5
HIS HANDS (125)

CHAPTER 6
A TEST OF FAITH (141)

CHAPTER 7
GOD'S WILL (195)

ACKNOWLEDGMENTS

It's not easy reliving mistakes from the past but sometimes it is necessary in order to move forward. Our past does not define who we are, nor does it dictate our future. Our past was designed to be a life lesson for us and a testimony to others, not a life sentence. Let us not be ashamed of our errors but allow them to guide and redirect others who are on their way to making those same mistakes. You never know how your testimony can impact someone else. This is why this autobiography was important for me.

With that said, I want to thank my parents Bobby Williams and Shirley Johnson as well as my sister Fhanta Williams for understanding the necessity of this journey and supporting it. Fhanta, you really touched me when you told me not to let anyone talk me out of telling my story even after you knew some of the things that I would be sharing about you. You and I are different in many ways but we will always be sisters and nothing on earth will ever change that.

Dasjuan, there is nothing like the bond of your first born son. To know that you have gone through so much and your life is just starting is heartbreaking. That's why your story was the hardest to write. I can't think about the events of February 2019 without getting emotional, but your words helped me get through. When I asked if you would be okay with me sharing your story, you told me that Jesus Christ was open with all that he went through and endured in life and on the Cross. You said that you are no better than Jesus. Those words helped me to push through so thank you. I love you.

To my cousins Dwight Follins and Melynda Rackley, I bet you didn't know that you were a part of God's Will when it came to me writing my story. Guess what, neither did I but I thank you two very much for being in place at the right time because without you, this book would still probably be just floating thoughts. Grandma Dot would be so proud of you two.
I love you all and I thank you.

THE BEGINNING

I was born June 23, 1978 in Deland, Florida to Robert and Shirley Williams. My dad named me Aishia after Stevie Wonder's daughter. He would sing *Isn't She Lovely* by Stevie Wonder to me all the time and always reminded me that I was created from love. He wanted my middle name to be Kabeebee Dada. My Grandmother, on the other hand, was not having it. She said to my dad, "You will not name my grandbaby that!"

He asked her, "What do you want to name her?"

She wanted to name me Nikkia. I don't know if she knew this at the time, but Nikkia means victorious. He has always had a soft spot for his mom and couldn't tell her no. As beautiful and sweet as she is, I don't think anyone can tell her no.

He was big on African names because he wanted us to understand our African roots. Born in the 1960's, my father's generation was just coming out of that slave mentality. They were looking for their own identity. They went from being identified as colored people to being called Afro Americans. During that time, they stopped putting chemicals in their hair and went natural. They also wanted to give their children African names to break away from slave names. My dad wanted his children to be proud of their heritage. He knew that our looks would be confusing to people because of our different features. We have eight different nationalities, African (Fulani Tribe), Asian (Filipino), German, Indian (not sure of the tribe), African American, Jamaican, Irish and French Canadian. It wasn't until my dad's generation transitioned from being called Black to African Americans that they realized they were not well-informed on the names they were giving their children. They were giving their offspring Arabic names. So, my name is Arabic which means alive and well. I prefer to use the Swahili meaning for my name. If spelled Aisha (Swahili), my name would mean Life. Well, I guess it's pretty much the same thing. The Swahili version gives more definition to who Aishia Nikkia is, a woman who lives life victoriously.

I weighed eight pounds and five ounces, looking like a china doll with slits for eyes. My hair was straight, dark, and covered the whole of my head. It was clear that I had some type of Asian in me. The older I got, the more those baby rolls came in, making me resemble the Michelin Tire Man. The thought still makes me smile now. I also had a small nose with no bridge and little nostrils. With my weight and nose, I quickly earned the nickname Piggy.

My hair grew long and wavy over the years although I prefer to wear it straight. That came from my paternal side. All of my aunts have long beautiful hair and my uncles have thick curly hair. They have what's called the natural soul glow.

I am the third oldest on both sides; my mom had two children from prior relationships, as did my dad. However, I am the firstborn from my parent's union. Even though they had five kids combined, my dad never ceased to let me know how special I was.

One day when I was small, my dad sat me on his lap, looked in my eyes and said, "Promise me that you will never cut your hair."

I looked back at him and said, "I promise."

To this day, that promise remains intact.

Unfortunately, my dad hasn't always been the person he is today. He was, as they would say back then, "God's gift to women." Or should I say, "A rolling stone." He was this short, chocolate mocha guy with all the perfect features. His eyes were slanted, his hair was loosely curled with a long rat tail that hung down the middle of his back. His build was muscular like Leroy Green on the Last Dragon. People jokingly compare him to the 1950's teen idol, Frankie Lymon; both of them had curly hair, beautiful brown skin that looked soft to touch, and slanted eyes, even though my dad's eyes are smaller. To me, there is no comparison. It's funny to listen to people trying to categorize his race. I like hearing people ask "What you is?" That's the southern slang for, What are you mixed with? All of our blood is tainted. Yet, people are surprised to hear that he identifies as black because his mother and father are African American. With his looks, smarts, and smooth talk, women flocked to him like crows to death.

My mom, on the other hand, is a beautiful country girl from Deland, Florida. She is average height, had a light brown complexion, high cheekbones, big beautiful light brown eyes, and shoulder length hair. I've heard people compare her to Lisa Raye but with round eyes. Again, to me, no one compared to my mom's beauty.

My parents first locked eyes while she was working at Winn-Dixie in DeLand. My dad and uncle Tony were talking about my mom's beauty when my uncle challenged my dad to get her number. He thought my mom was out of my dad's league because she was "so fine."

My dad responded, "Watch me."

He walked up to her and introduced himself. She excused herself, went inside of the walk-in freezer section and screamed. She then came back out, and they exchanged numbers. Needless to say, they went out on a few dates. His weakness has always been women, but he has never met anyone like my mom before. He had bit off more than he could chew with Mom because she was different. She stole his heart; before long, they were married and started a family. They moved to Jacksonville in 1977 to find answers about my mom's family that she was seeking. They traveled back and forth from Jacksonville to DeLand often which is why I was born there.

My dad was a poet. He always has the perfect words to say. When they were en route moving to Houston, Tx he made up a few songs about me. One was *Little Miss Mush Tush* which is a nickname he has for me. I was told that as a baby, my face would glow. I'd have the biggest grin when he started singing that song to me as I'd jump up and down with joy while he was holding me. The other song that he made for me is called Daddy's Little Girl. This is my favorite because he would sing this song to me throughout the years, even in my adult years. It goes:

> Daddy's little baby laying here in my arms
> Showing me your charms
> Daddy's little girl.
> What you gonna do when you feel all grown up,
> First day of school, will you live by the rule?

Learn to play, play to learn, are you going to stay?

Will you get an A?

Daddy's little girl.

Daddy's little baby laying here in my arms,

Showing me your charms,

Daddy's little girl.

How you gon'na feel on graduation day?

The world is in your hands,

How you gon'na feel?

When he ask me for your hand what I'm gon'na say?

He's taking you away,

Daddy's little girl.

Daddy won't have baby laying here in my arms,

Showing me your charms,

Daddy's little girl.

Daddy's little baby laying here in my arms,

Showing me your charms,

Da-dee's Lit-tle Gurllll, Toot Toot!

This song reminds me that no matter how old I get, I will always be daddy's little girl. When I was old enough to speak and would ask about his day, he would tell me that it is better now that he's in my presence.

One time he said to me, "Do you see the rain outside? The drops that you can count amount to the love you have for me. The ones that you can't count, that amounts to the love I have for you."

And to this day, those words remind me that if no one else loves me, Daddy does. These words drew me closer and closer to my father, because they were said with heartfelt compassion. Even today, I know he means every word he speaks to me.

Texas didn't work out for my parents and they moved back to Jacksonville within about a month or so of arriving. A year after I was born, my mom got pregnant again. It was a girl! My dad named her Fhanta Fatima. My mom had two children prior to us, Natahsha, who we call Tot because my maternal great-grandmother, Estelle, would say that my sister was her little Tater Tot, and Charles. Tot and I are four years apart, while Charles and I are two. Since the family was growing, my parents decided to move to the Riverside area. At this time in the eighties, Riverside was a predominantly mixed neighborhood. It was pretty quiet until the drugs rolled in. I can still remember the address where we lived, 2337 College Street. This was the perfect house for us. The house was two stories with a fence surrounding it. My dad had duct taped one of the oak trees in the back and gave it arms and legs. He used this as his martial arts training dummy, and every morning at sunrise, he would go outside and train with it. We also had an exit to the alley in the back where we would take a short cut to the neighborhood store.

There was an oak tree next to the house which was so close that we could reach it from our bedroom window. My sister

Fhanta and I were tomboys. We liked wrestling instead of playing with dolls, chilling with boys, and climbing trees. Once, Fhanta got stuck in that tree and called out for Popeye to come and save her. We joke with her about that to this day. Tot was more feminine. However, while we used the oak tree to climb on, Tot was using it to sneak out of the house. I don't recall her ever getting caught. I was on the lookout for her most of the time.

In the front yard was a beautiful date tree. My dad would use those dates to make wine with. It was also at this house where my dad did a backflip over his Toronado. Not one part of his body touched the steel. Not even the long rat tail that hung low down his back. He was skilled at backflipping. I was recently reminded by my cousins Dwight and Ernestco about how my dad flipped over a fence once without touching it. Everyone thought he was a ninja. To me, Dad was my superhero.

The inside of our house was pretty cool for the eighties. Our living room décor was brown, gold, and brass. There were brass elephants, storks, and a gold antique table that sat in the center of the living room along with two end tables. My favorite was the vintage gold and cream rotary phone with the twenty-inch cord. I used to unscrew the ear and mouthpiece just to play with them and then put them back together before I got caught.

My dad was a martial artist and studied Gung Fu. He fancied himself after Bruce Lee. He also had a dojo and would fight in tournaments against the best. Hanging on the living room walls were swords, nunchucks, medals, and certificates from my dad's martial arts achievements. The trophies from those tournaments stood very tall from the floor near the couch. They stood almost as tall as I was. Upstairs were the bedrooms and the second bathroom. Tot's room was lavender. That was her favorite color. Guess what, she grew up and married a guy named Lavander. How ironic is that!

Then there was Mom and Dad's room. It was cool because they had a mirrored sliding closet door. Inside were the coolest clothes and the finest furs. They even had a waterbed! My siblings and I loved to make waves with our bodies on that bed. Our room was pink. My brother Kahlil came three years after Fhanta. That's when dad decided to build a three-way bunk bed. I had the top bunk, and Fhanta had the middle. They were built directly under each other. Kahlil's was still connected but came out on the side and touched the floor.

The stairway was one of the places where I have one of my best memories. You see, my sister Fhanta was very sneaky but good at playing innocent. She played right into my mom's hands and my other siblings knew it. Her strength was, "Never let them see you sweat." Because of that, we played on it.

One day Fhanta was thirsty. My mischievous brother, Charles, was drinking Mellow Yellow soda from a glass bottle. He had just finished it but decided to prank her and pee into the bottle. He then gave it to her to drink. She sipped; we all watched, grinning in anticipation. Charles told us what he was going to do before he did it so Tot was peeking from the bathroom adjacent to the stairs. I had walked slowly down the stairs passing Fhanta when he called her and offered her a drink. After her first sip, we were shocked that she couldn't tell what it was. We didn't think she'd actually go for it! Charles told her that it was pee.

She said, "So. It tasted good."

We were like "Ewwww!". We knew she didn't mean it but that Fhanta wasn't going to let us know that we had gotten the best of her.

Despite Fhanta getting us in trouble and us getting her back, it was like we were the perfect family. When our parents would take us to McDonald's or any other drive-up restaurant, Mom would totally change her voice at the speaker. It was so funny. She would speak in a made up language. It would sound like a mixture of different languages all at once. The workers would ask for a translator. She would pull up to the window and then self-translate. It was hilarious! It made the workers' day, too.

On the outside, no one knew that trouble was brewing in paradise. The only thing that we kids saw was nothing but pure love from our parents. We never heard the arguments; we never saw the struggles. Love was poured into us from everywhere. My dad's friends treated us like daughters. We also had so much love from both sides of the family. My aunt Dot, who we called, grandma Dot would often have gatherings at her house; boy, could she cook! I don't know why we called our aunt, grandma. Maybe because we didn't know much about my mom's family so we followed suit with what our cousins were calling her. Regardless, she accepted it with love and no one corrected us. The paternal side of my family lived in Philadelphia, but when they came down for a visit, they always brought our favorite, Tasty Cakes! At the time, we didn't have them in Jacksonville so they were sure to bring them for us with every visit because they knew we loved them. My favorite was the Butterscotch Crumpets. Yum! They treated us as if we were their own children. I remember my dad telling me that family is everything. This is probably how I became so family oriented. Maybe this is why I became the protector of the family as well. Although all my siblings were tough and could physically defend themselves, anyone who said anything about them had to deal with me. I didn't care how much we despised each other that day; those were my siblings, and only I could feel ill about them.

I remember when my dad bought my mom a brand-new Oldsmobile Tornado. Someone decided to pilfer it, which was the worst mistake of their life. My dad had completed his own investigation, tracked down the thief, and went to his door. He wasn't home. Dressed in a ninja-yoroi, Daddy had waited in the tree next to the man's home until he arrived. As day turned to night, the crook finally made it home. As he walked down the sidewalk, my dad jumped out of the tree and attacked him. This thief had a large muscular build and was also skilled in martial arts, but he was no match for Robert Earl who was slim and short. Daddy beat this man to a pulp. Word got out about my dad, and everyone knew not to mess with him or his family.

Growing up, there were plenty of times when we didn't have food to eat. I didn't know this then, but I found out later that when I thought Dad was treating us to those rare delicacies, we were actually having a food shortage. One Thanksgiving, we didn't have any food, but it was tradition for us to have a family meal around the table. We lived up the street from a duck pond. So, my dad went there, grabbed ducks, killed them, and brought them back home for us to eat. We had no idea that this was the reason why.

There were also times when we had deer and gophers. That's because Dad went on the hunt for his family. Another memory that I'll never forget is the one of my parents and my mom's rabbit, Inky. My dad told Inky and my mom that if he ever bit him then he would bite him back. Well, it happened. My dad went to grab Inky and he bit my dad. My dad kept his word. Mom came home one day after work. We sat down to eat dinner at the table as a family. It was customary for Inky to greet mom when she walked in but this day, there was no sign of him.

"Where's Inky?" she asked.

My dad looked at her with the "Oops" face.

Mom's countenance fell. She then said in her saddest

voice, "Bob, I know you didn't."

He slowly nodded his head yes as he grinned, followed by a burst of laughter. Mom was sick to her stomach. She was hurt! She felt betrayed. To make matters worse, my dad had gotten on the phone, told his buddies what he did, and invited them over for dinner for the next day. Mom wasn't having it. When his buddies came the following day, they were excited to taste this rabbit that my dad had bragged about. My dad went into the refrigerator and grabbed the foil-covered pan that contained the half-eaten rabbit. To his dismay, Inky was stuffed with flies.

See, Mom was a prankster herself. Mom was determined not to have anyone else eat her rabbit. So, she collected all the flies from the windowsill and stuffed the rabbit with them. Mom had the last laugh. Mom fought back smartly.

I have great parents, but Dad was more of a fun parent. One time he pretended that he was dead and did such a good job at it, too. No matter how much tickling, kicking, punching, or pushing we did, he didn't move. I guess by him being a martial artist, that didn't faze him. I was starting to become worried. Tot was not having it. She was smart. She went and got an ice cube and rubbed it down his spine. He jumped up so quickly! You can't fake past freezing, especially when playing with the spine. We all cracked up, even Mom.

Dad was also our safety net. In Riverside, a menace

named the Riverside Rapist was assaulting women in the neighborhood. One of us had called Mom from work and told her that someone with pantyhose on his head was trying to break into our house, based on what Fhanta told us. Mom was working as a loan processor at the mortgage company, Stockton, Whatley, Davin & Company; she couldn't take off from work, so she called my dad whose job was more flexible. Dad came home immediately and scoured the neighborhood. He also looked for signs of break-in through our burglar bars. After there were no signs of a break-in, Dad lined us up and told us to spill the truth. It became a he-said, she-said game as Fhanta reneged on what she had told us.

Dad threatened to whip everyone until he got the truth out. We begged Fhanta to tell the truth, but she wouldn't. Dad took us up to the room. The sound of the whip of the belt followed by the cries, I was scared! Then it was my turn.

I pleaded, "Dad, I'm telling the truth. Fhanta told us about the pantyhose man."

Dad said, "I believe you, but I have to do this to get my point across," he continued, "I'm going to strike the bed. I need you to fake cry and make it as believable as possible. Can you do that?"

"Yes, sir!" I acquiesced as I began my performance.

I don't know about my other siblings, but I do know that I got off scot-free. I also know they were upset at her after that.

The next time she said that someone with pantyhose was looking through our window, it wasn't taken seriously. However, Mom heard something which was evident enough for her to go and check it out with the gun my dad had bought her. To her surprise, it was the pantyhose man trying to break into our house.

Dad wasn't there, but Mom cocked that gun and exclaimed, "Freeze sucker!"

She held him there until the police arrived.

Mom and Dad were just the perfect duo. They were Robert Earl and Shirl the Pearl. Both of my parents had beautiful voices. They would sing with such passion and love in their eyes. That talent was passed to all of my siblings. I remember when I was in the car singing and thought no one was listening. Fhanta was in the back seat. I can't remember which sibling was in the front, although I believe it was Tot. My eyes were closed, my head was going from side to side, and I was getting into it. Mom turned the radio up. As the music got louder, so did I.

I guess she had heard enough, because her next words were, "Ewww! Who is that?"

Did I mention that the gift of singing skipped me? Man, I have never been so embarrassed! Fhanta pointed directly to me as she snickered. Everyone in the car was laughing. I didn't find it funny. I just slouched in my seat and shut up for the rest of the ride. My self-confidence was shattered from that day forward.

My dad, on the other hand, when he was around, made

me feel like I could do anything and be whoever I wanted to be. I will never forget the time when I wanted to compete in a track competition. My mom knew I was no good and didn't want me to go out there and embarrass myself.

But I was determined that I could compete and win, so my dad said to my mom, "If she thinks she can do it, let her."

I went out there in my professional pose. I looked the part, and I was ready. The gun sounded, and the runners took off! There I was, running.

I was so fast! Well, at least in my mind. I noticed that everyone was in front of me, and no one was behind me. I was running with my hands locked tight trailing behind my body. I finally passed my parents. I looked up at the stands, and guess who was cheering me on with a big smile on his face: Daddy! Mom was embarrassed for me, though. She did tell me that she was proud that I didn't quit; Dad grabbed me at the finish line, gave me a big hug, and told me how proud he was. It was different. Mom's tone may have been candid, whereas Dad's was more celebratory.

Dad was always telling me how smart I was. If I failed at something, he would have ways of uplifting me instead of putting me down; he would show me a better way of doing things. He would provide any knowledge he had until I understood, whether it was an example, solution, feedback, or an experience. It was always tactful and in a loving manner, too. Mom meant well, but that just wasn't her specialty. This is why, no matter what Dad did, he could never do any wrong in my eyes.

One peaceful night, my younger siblings and I were worn out from the day. Fhanta and Kahlil wanted to sleep in my top bunk that night, so I let them. In the middle of the night, I was awakened by a light noise. I opened my eyes and saw my dad's silhouette. He had snuck a family member into our room and had sex with her on my brother's bed. I was crushed! My mom and my older siblings were in their rooms that were close by.

I told myself that my dad was still my hero. To me, he could do no wrong. So I sucked it up, pretended I didn't see anything, and kept it a secret until I was grown with children. Until now, the only people who knew that I saw what happened were those involved. I'm not sure how Mom found out, but it wasn't by me. She has always been a smart woman.

I overheard her say, "Not again! This time you crossed the line."

This told me it wasn't the first time he had messed around on her. She was clearly done.

I was eight years old. This was it! My world was about to crash! Mom and Dad had been on the brink of a divorce for a while obviously, according to her. But they loved each other too much to actually see it through. This particular night, everything came to a head.

Mom finally said those two dreadful words, "I'm done."

The very thought of the duo, Robert Earl and Shirl the Pearl, no longer being an item shattered his world so much so that he wanted to take his life. He walked into his room and grabbed his gun. The next thing I knew, Mom was rushing my siblings and I out the door. She ran to our neighbor, Mr. Kimble, and told him what was happening. Mr. Kimble convinced mom to stay outside, as he was concerned for her safety. As the two of them were talking, trying to figure out a game plan, a single gunshot was heard from outside.

Mom screamed as Mr. Kimble tried to comfort her. She wouldn't let him, but she did tell him to watch us while she fearfully went in to check out the scene. To her dismay, Dad was alive and unharmed. He had fired a single shot into the ceiling. Mom was rightfully outraged! Not that she wanted him to take his life, but this scheme was atrocious. And just like that, Dad was gone. The next thing I knew, he had moved back to Philadelphia. I just cried. All I could think was my daddy is gone. Who was going to protect us now? Well, when my parents split, so did our security.

So now, this beautiful single mother was doing her best to raise five children on her own. Tot began acting out; I guess she was dealing with her own trauma the best way she knew how. She ran away a couple of times and would do things that most teenagers would do. My brother Charles was a bit impish. He would do things like poke Tot's parrot, Charlie, in the throat with a broomstick until it said his name. It eventually croaked. He also liked to play with fire. It was all fun games until he burned my mom's rug and almost set the house aflame.

Shortly after that incident, he disappeared. I asked my mom where he was. She said his dad kidnapped him. I remember crying and begging her to go get him. She gave different excuses as to why she couldn't; eventually, she said he would have a better life living with his dad. I was really close to both Tot and Charles, but Tot was my rider. She and I did everything together. I looked up to her. When she was upset about something, so was I.

There was one particular incident when Tot got upset with Fhanta. It felt like mom looked at us older three children as troublemakers and Fhanta and Kahlil as saints.

For me, my only crime was "being just like your daddy," as mom would say.

Well, Fhanta was really no saint. She was just too smart to get caught with her wrongdoings. She was the sneaky type, whereas we were out in the open with whatever we did. On this day, Mom had told everyone to clean up. Fhanta decided she didn't want to. Tot told on her. Mom didn't do anything about it, so Tot confronted her. Fhanta got upset and spit on her. Before you knew it, Tot hauled off and punched her in the face. Guess what followed. Yep, a punch from me, too. Right as Fhanta was standing on top of the plinth. Some may say I was wrong but I was protective over my big sister.

Next thing I knew, my grandma Dot passed away and we were no longer visiting my maternal side of the family. I don't know what caused the separation because mom was good with keeping kids out of grown folks business. It wasn't until we were grown and had kids that we reunited with them again. Dad was still in Philadelphia, so our only contact with him was by phone. I would cry every time I heard his voice.

There weren't many kids around my age in the neighborhood that I could talk to; my childhood best friend, Mandy, was the only other female that I hung around besides my sisters. The rest of our friends were males. So, quite naturally, I grew up being a tomboy. Besides, I didn't want to get caught up in the stereotype of "being cute," as this was something that I heard quite often that had a negative connotation. As a matter of fact, females wanted to fight me, even in elementary school. They said I thought I was cute, because I was light skinned with long hair. My looks were not a threat to Mandy though. She was beautiful, too. She was tall, had a beautiful brown complexion, and was very confident. So confident that we fought over more pressing matters, like whose breasts were bigger (even though both of us only had nubs). So, after my parents split, I spent more time with Mandy.

One of our favorite things to do was to go to Pop's, the corner store. There, we played arcade games and ate food. We also bought candy and soda there. Going to Pop's was the perfect getaway for kids to clear their minds and stay out of trouble. And that's what we did.

One day, on the way home from Pops, Mandy had gone her way and I, mine. I walked in the door and was greeted by the lovely Ms. R. She and my mom were best friends. After my parents split, Ms. R would frequent our home more often. The two of them watched Soap Operas daily and ate crab on the weekends. Ms. R had a son that I will call, Kae. He and I were also the same age, so it wasn't out of the ordinary for him to come play with my sister and me. Besides, there weren't many kids in the neighborhood. Kae came to our house looking for his mom.

By this time, I was hanging out in my fenced-in backyard. I guess our parents had told him I was back there. He came to see me. We talked about the divorce and what happened the night that my father shot into the ceiling.

Then he said, "Hey, let's try something."

"Try what?" I asked.

He had the audacity to ask me to suck his penis. I told him that it was gross and that I wasn't going to do it. He tried hard to convince me and then begged.

Eventually, I gave in. Right there on the opposite side of my fence, at eight years old, I had my first sexual experience. I did not like it. I remember going straight home to my room feeling nasty. I felt that I had no one to talk to; after all, it was my fault for giving in.

Some time later, I was in school. I attended Central Riverside Elementary. I remember leaving class to go to the restroom. As I walked out of the stall; a girl greeted me with small talk and then asked me to suck on her breast.

Once again, I found that utterly disgusting, and of course I said, "No!"

Words were exchanged, then she told me she would meet me outside at 3:00 when school let out. I was ready. She must have told her friends that she was going to whip my tail because there was a crowd standing outside waiting.

She walked up to me and said, "Talk that mess now!"

This was followed by a two-handed push to the chest.

I swung on her, and it was on! We were going at it! I must have been kicking her butt because the next thing I knew, her brother jumped in the fight. Then my little brother, Kahlil jumped in. Fhanta joined in after that. Victory was ours! It was Bailey's versus Williams'. Sure, they were outnumbered; had they left the fight fair, it wouldn't have been an issue. I couldn't help but think about little Ms. Bailey over the years. I figured she must have had a traumatic experience such as being raped or molested; perhaps that was her way of reaching out. I felt bad for her for years.

We eventually moved from College Street when I was in the fifth grade. I was happy to leave behind the constant reminders of guilt, embarrassment, and bad memories although I loved that house. Over the years, I would have dreams about it. It wasn't until I confronted the ghost of the past that 2337 College Street went away from my dreams.

    We were at a new house; I went to a new school finishing up my fifth grade year at Mary McCleod Bethune Elementary, and I had new friends. Everything seemed grand except the relationship between my mom and me. I didn't understand the pain she was going through being a single mom. Her oldest son was living across the country in California. Her oldest daughter was a rebellious teen. And the only thing that mattered to me was that I was that my point got across. Because I was so vocal, Mom didn't hesitate to remind me how much I was just like my father. After a while, I began to see this as a compliment instead of criticism. Still, my father could do no wrong. I must admit, the smarter my dad got, the more arrogant he became. Still, one couldn't help but admire his wisdom. He was still a charmer and no matter what he was to other people -good or bad- he was still my hero. The truth of the matter was, I had my dad's mouth and his stubbornness but not his arrogance. I stood up for what I believed was right, and no one could stray me from that.

When it came down to defending myself though, I was inadequate. Physically, I had the hands to defend myself even though I didn't always want to. However, I had yet to develop my mental strength. I remember my sixth grade year. I went to

S.P. Livingston when it was just a sixth grade center. I was shy and used to walk with my head turned to the side. I also used to stay to myself. This caught the attention of a girl named Erica Ellis. She was another one who said "I think I'm cute.". She would bully me like she was getting paid to do it and, like a dummy, I let her. I wasn't scared to fight her; I just did not want to get in trouble at home. Momma made it very clear that if we misbehaved in school, the consequences at home would be worse. When Dad was there, she'd make him be the punisher. This was cool, because he didn't like whipping us. He'd whip the bed a lot of times and told us to pretend like we were crying. If we got whipped, it was because we really deserved it. Mom, on the other hand, didn't let up on us. She wasn't trying to hear it and neither was I, so I just took the persecution.

One day, I had my head down on the desk, and Erica came by and pushed her fingers in my head. I jumped up as if I was going to do something. To be honest, I didn't know what I was going to do at that moment, but she threw me off with her reaction.

"Are you going to tell?" she asked in a scared voice.

I looked at her for a second and then said no. I walked out of the classroom and went to the bathroom to get myself together. It was at that moment that I realized that people only do what you allowed them to do to you. From that moment on, I had made up my mind that I would never be bullied again. She didn't try again after that, but she's part of the reason why I cannot stand bullies. I stand up to them at any cost.

I was retained that year. It was not that I didn't know my work, but I just wasn't doing it. I was transferred to J.E.B. Stuart Middle School. This was a center for grades six through eight. I was a bus rider even though the school was only a few miles from the house. One day as I was riding the bus, a new girl got on. She was beautiful with long wavy hair. She had a light complexion. She was really quiet and stayed to herself. She sat behind me on the bus this particular day. Someone from the back started calling her names and throwing paper at her while others were laughing. She sat there and just took it. I knew exactly what she was going through, and I'd had enough of watching her being tormented.

I jumped up out of my seat and said, "Let another person mess with her! If you mess with her, you mess with me. And believe me, that's not what you want!"

The bus grew silent. She smiled. They left her alone. We ended up getting off at the same stop. I found out that her name is Lisa Blake. She had just moved here from Rhode Island and hadn't made any friends yet. So, I was her first friend. Lisa and I were inseparable. Her mom, Ms. Irma was super sweet and could cook her butt off. My favorite dish that she made was curry and roti. She also had two brothers, Ronald and Al. They were my family away from family. They eventually moved back to Rhode Island. I was so hurt when she left, but she and I remain sisters to this day. After Lisa, I started hanging tight with a girl named Tiffany. Tiffany loved sports, particularly basketball. She had collections of all the basketball greats combined in several binders from Larry Bird, Kareem Abdul-Jabbar, Wilt Chamberlain, Hakeem Olajuwon, Michael Jordan, Scottie Pippen, and many, many more. She knew so much about the sport, she could have been the assistant coach. I became fascinated with her knowledge which is how I got into the game. One day, Tiffany and I decided to go to K-Mart on Blanding to pick up a few things. As we got closer, she told me that she was going to steal from the store. I asked her how she would do that? She said she tries the clothes on, layers up, and then walks out.

"You don't get scared you're going to get caught?"

She quipped, "No, are you going to try?"

"Yeah."

We walked in and she said, "Just be cool."

Because I had on a fitted dress, I decided to go for the bodycon style in my size. I grabbed about two or three of these dresses and walked out. To my surprise, we walked out of the door with no issues.

"I told you," she grinned.

I had no fear. I wanted to go back. She told me to wait so I wouldn't become a known face. This was something we did often. One day, I went in and racked up on clothes, underwear, and bras. Then I walked out.

Right behind me, just past the automatic doors, was a security guard dressed in regular clothes. He was watching and following me the whole time.

"Miss, I need you to come with me."

I was caught! I was nervous, not for what I had just done but for getting caught. My mom was going to kill me! They had a female officer come in and search me, and there they were: all of the items that I had nabbed. They kept me in the back office as they made that dreadful call to my mother. She must have been livid because she didn't drive to come get me. It was only one and a half miles from where we lived, but the walk back was like walking the green mile.

It was pure silence until someone from the opposite side of the street spoke to me.

"Hey Aishia," they said in an excited tone.

My mom replied, "She just got caught stealing!"

That was more embarrassing than anything that I've ever encountered. To this day, I never found out who was speaking to me. I never stole in that nature again. My mom told me that she was going to send me to go stay with my dad for the summer. I was ecstatic.

Before I left, I wanted to see my boyfriend, Tim Taylor. I was in middle school, and he was in high school. He was my trophy only for that reason. Tot dated his brother Steve, so I had easy access to him. I told my mom I wanted to stay the weekend with my sister. She was glad to get me out of her hair.

Tim stayed the night, too. We had our own room at her house, and we were getting busy! He was on top of me. Then I was on him. As I was riding him, we both were moaning and sweating.

He spoke out, "Oh, Fhanta!"

It was like a record had just been scratched! I just stopped and stared into his eyes as he tried to correct himself.

"What's wrong, Nikki?" he asked, calling me by my nickname (which was what most people called me back then).

"Don't play with me," I said.

Then this joker had the audacity to ask me to make him a peanut butter and jelly sandwich. Once again, I paused and with an attitude, I got up. Like a good girlfriend, I made the sandwich. He had no idea that the bread landed on the floor first. What hurt even more than him calling me by my sister's name during that intimate moment was that my sister had always made me feel like I was her competition instead of her sister. She always wanted to be better than me in everything growing up. I think it bothered her that I was older. I didn't know if they had actually slept together or if it was his fantasy. I knew I'd never get the truth if I asked, so I never gave her the satisfaction of mentioning it. Needless to say, that was the last time I talked to Tim.

I wasn't happy about going back home either because I didn't know what to think of my sister. On my bedroom wall, I had this Oscar the grouch "To Do" poster pinned up facing my pink canopy bed. It had a clean panty liner that I had slapped across its mouth one day when I was upset with my mother, that I had never taken down. All I could do at that moment was stare at that poster with tears in my eyes, chewing gum until I fell asleep. When I woke up, there was gum stuck in my hair. My mom's boyfriend Ernie was this big Goldmouth looking dude (from the movie Life) that I didn't care too much for. She eventually married him. He cut the gum out of my hair and left a small patch at the front of my head. I was upset and crying!

My mom said it would grow back. That didn't matter. What mattered was what was missing in that moment, my hair!

I swear this man didn't like me. I recall a time when I was washing clothes; his slippers were in the laundry room so I washed them.

This joker asked, "Who washed my slippers?"

"I did. They were in the laundry room, so I assumed they were dirty," I said.

Ernie jacked me up to the point that my feet were off the ground. He told me to never wash his slippers again. I swung, and he let me down. I ran in the room to tell Kahlil and Fhanta. These crazies were laughing about the fact I had even attempted to swing on him. We kept the jokes coming when it came to Ernie.

One summer, Charles was home visiting, as was customary. I remember someone walking in on Ernie and mom being intimate. Gross! The thought of that was disgusting! You had this beautiful, fragile, drop dead gorgeous model and then this man who looked like his only job was to steal inmates' cornbread at the lunch table together; being one. The thought of it makes me cringe.

In an outburst, Charles exclaimed, "So you saw his weenie do?"

We all were like, "What's a weenie do?"

He said "It's when your stomach sticks out further than your weenie do!"

Man, we fell out! What made it funny was that he had this big stomach and although no one wanted to visualize his weenie, we couldn't help but continue the jokes with descriptions. I was happy their marriage didn't last long.

I eventually left to spend time with my dad in Philadelphia. I was having a ball! He asked me if I wanted to spend time with my sister. Of course, I did! She was living with her mom who had a few people inside her home at the time.

As I was sleeping, I felt someone's hands on my breast. I woke up like what the heck!

I don't quite remember the conversation but it kind of went something like, "Go with the flow."

I remember feeling scared and nervous but I sucked it up. This seemed to be my go-to survival response: just go with the flow and pretend.

When I went back to my dad's the next day, I said nothing. I remember my dad asking if I was okay and I told him I was tired. I tried not to let it ruin my time with my dad. My dad loves telling stories. As a matter of fact, he is one of the greatest, most animated storytellers of all time so being around him makes it easier to escape any negativity that I had faced. I continued the rest of the summer with him until the day my sister Mya was born. We didn't know she was coming that day. As a matter of fact, Dad was on his way to take me to the airport until he received the call. We stopped in for a brief visit so that he could be there for her birth. I was fortunate to be able to see her; even if it was just for a split second.

As I reflect back on my teenage years, I see that I experienced some emotional rollercoasters and maybe some cliffs that could have taken me over the edge, but they weren't all bad. My mom had started to link up with her sister Norma. She lived in Bunnell, FL with her family. We traveled there often to spend time with them after they reunited. She lived with her husband, my Uncle Ricky, and their daughter, Rochelle. Once Rochelle and I hung out that first time, we became inseparable. We would visit her just about every break. There wasn't anything that we didn't talk or laugh about. Rochelle felt my pain when it came to Fhanta. Fhanta would act so ditsy that we started calling her Sinclair, the character from the television show *Living Single*.

In no time, Rochelle became more of a sister than a cousin.

Then, my paternal cousin, Renny came down to Florida to stay with us for a while. The family calls him Ren for short. At this time, Ren's bond was tighter with me than my other siblings. He and I loved the group A Tribe Called Quest and were bumping *The Low End Theory* album hard! One of our favorite jams is called "What." The rap repeats the words *"What to go"* seven times before shouting the final "What!" But it sounds like they are repeating the words Whatchigga. It was because of that song that we would always be the Whatchiggas. To this day, that is how we refer to each other.

Ren taught me how to dive off a diving board, and when I needed to talk about anything, I would either go to Ren or Rochelle or both. They always had my back. Before Ren and Rochelle, it was just me and my dog, Beethoven. My mom had given him to us one day, and I took over. He stayed in my room, and I did everything the owner was supposed to do.

One day I snuck a boy into my room from my window. Ren came knocking at my door, so I made my friend go under the bed. I then stuffed some clothes and sheets under the bed to hide him. After Ren walked in, Beethoven decided he wanted to tell on me. He started grabbing the sheets from under the bed. Ren saw the guy so of course he had to come out of hiding. Luckily, it was just Ren; of course, he wasn't snitching. We just laughed about it as my friend came scooting out from under the bed. Obviously, we called Rochelle and told her about it. We were a trio until Ren had to go back to Philly.

School was back in. I was in the seventh grade. We moved to a different neighborhood again. I swear we moved as if we were in witness protection or something. I now attended Jefferson Davis Middle School. It was there that I opened up a bit and expanded my friend base, but my focus was far from my schoolwork. I learned how to play Tonk and Spades; gambling at school was my thing. We would play cards at the gym, in the classroom when the teacher wasn't looking, at the bus stop, or wherever we could get it in.

Needless to say, I was left behind again and guess what, we moved again. The good thing about us moving so much was that I never had to face the embarrassment of my peers seeing me being left behind.

This time I went to Stillwell Middle. I was the new girl there. It was there that I met my best friend, Kutana. People feared her and her sisters. She and I just clicked from day one. We were two peas in a pod. She was my rider and I was hers. We lived by the motto: "Act first, ask questions later." If she fought, I was there and if I fought, she was there. I remember one day our sisters were on the bus, and they fought each other. We both looked at each other like *Please don't do it*, and we let them have their fair fight.

We talked about everything, too! One day I decided to skip school, and I went back home. Nathaniel Clark, a brother from my mom's Kingdom Hall, must have seen me walking back home, because he came to our house shortly after. He knocked on the door.

"Is your mom home?" he asked.

"No, she isn't, she's at work," I replied.

He sat down on the couch and asked me to sit on his lap. Reluctantly, I complied. He started rubbing on my breasts. I froze.

I can't tell you the conversation that took place after that, because I was in shock. I couldn't believe a Jehovah's Witness was sitting in my house molesting me. Once again, I believed it was my fault, because had I been in school, it wouldn't have happened. I went back to school the next day and didn't even tell my bestie what had happened. My grades were dropping significantly. I would go to school, fight, get suspended, come back to school, and do it again. I remember one time coming off suspension to fight a girl because people said that we looked alike. I could not stand for people to confuse us because we look nothing alike. I had told my friends that I was going to fight her. One day I saw her in the cafeteria. My friends looked at me like what are you going to do? I couldn't back down so I walked up to her. I gave her a little push to get the fight started but she pushed me back with all her might. I fell into the trash can that was behind me. I got up swinging! I felt like I was winning the fight, even though I wasn't putting my all into it. The school's security officer came along with the principal, Mr. Turner, to break up the fight. I didn't like the way the guard grabbed me and apparently, I was being too wild because he slammed me on the floor. When the 8th graders came in, some said that I had lost the fight but they only saw me being held down. I heard some of the 7th grade bystanders say that I won. I asked Kutana who won the fight. She flexed her muscles to say I did. I felt a little better because I knew she wouldn't lie to me. However, I was not happy that there was no clear winner. I said that I was fighting her again at the end of the school year and I guarantee there will be a clear winner. As the school year drew closer, I realized how stupid that fight was, so I decided to let it go.

My final grades were all F's and one D. My mom didn't even get upset, but she did tell me I was going to grow up to be a pretty little nothing; just a bag lady. That stung more than any punishment that she could have ever rendered. Still, I was getting comfortable with this person I was becoming.

I started working when I was eleven years old, starting with the Student Work Program. My sister and I would work there on and off until we were old enough to get a regular job. When I turned fourteen, I started working for Winn-Dixie as a bagger. My oldest sister, Tot and my mom couldn't wait for me to get home after my first day so that they could come with the jokes.

"I told you that you were going to end up being a bag lady," my mom said as my sister laughed.

"Yep, and I am making money doing it," I said in response.

I then told my mom that I wanted to buy a television with my first check. She asked where I was going to get it from. I told her I wanted to purchase it from Rent-A-Center. It was in a plaza only a few blocks down from Winn-Dixie. I had already scoped out the television that I wanted, and I was determined to get it.

Mom told me I was going to end up paying more money than what it was worth, but I didn't care. I wanted to feel accomplished.

So she said, "If that's what you want to do, it's your money. Do it."

That's exactly what I did. She took me to get the TV. It totaled about two hundred ninety dollars. It was twenty four dollars and some change per month that I had to pay. After paying the tv off, I paid close to four hundred dollars but didn't care. I purchased this with my money and it felt good. Me and my Beethoven would be chilling in the room looking at the TV and enjoying each other's company.

Not too long after I bought my TV, my mom decided to go out of town with her boyfriend to the Bethune Cookman and FAMU Classic. Tot came over to watch us for the weekend. I was in the eighth grade, dating this boy named David. We both loved the R&B group, Silk. He would be in my bedroom, and we would blast those songs while getting it on. Tot dated his cousin Gino. Gino spent the night while David went home. Everyone went to sleep. The house was quiet. I woke up to use the restroom and saw Tot and Gino knocked out in Mom's room on her bed. My room was diagonal to Mom's once you went through the living room.

I went back to sleep. The next thing you know I was awakened by a man's finger inside of my private area, followed by his penis. My sister's boyfriend was raping me! Once again, I froze. I pretended to sleep through it in fear of what could have happened if he found out that I was awake.

This time I told my sister Fhanta what happened. I found no consolation in telling her. She confided in me about something personal that she went through but it felt more like she was saying "suck it up, life sucks."

I then reached out to my cousin Rochelle and told her. She gave me some comfort and told me to tell my mom. I told her that she wouldn't believe me. Rochelle gave me the confidence I needed to go to my mom anyway.

Eventually, I did but I didn't tell her everything. I had just told her about Nathaniel and Gino. As expected Mom didn't believe me. I had no one to turn to. I was left to deal with everything by myself. I did see Nathaniel many years later. It was from a distance but I was close enough to recognize him, although he didn't see me. He was walking in the gas station on Wilson Blvd. If I remember correctly, he was in a mail truck. That part of my memory is slightly faded. But, it looked like the Mighty hand of

God had come down upon him. Whereas before, he appeared vibrant and full of life, this day he looked worn and tired; like life was beating him down. I was satisfied to see that honestly. I still wished Mom believed me. I knew the one person who would believe and protect me, I had to protect. My dad would have killed someone over me, but my dad was already in and out of jail from doing his own thing.

I could recall a time when my dad came to visit us here in Florida, and I went with him to Best Buy on Atlantic Boulevard. We had just gotten out of the vehicle when this white Navy man was walking toward his car. He accused me of hitting his car with my dad's car door. I politely told him that I didn't do it. As a matter of fact, even if I did, there was no way he could have seen it from the angle where he was at the time of the accusation. He became disrespectful.

My dad walked up to him and said "if she said she didn't hit the car then she didn't do it." Then, dad asked if they were going to have a problem. I had to convince my dad to walk away. I didn't want to be responsible for this man's life, because he clearly had no idea who he was up against. Luckily, my dad has always listened to me. He walked away.

Had I told Dad that someone had done something so cruel to me, I knew that his reaction would be the one time that I wouldn't be able to control. I didn't want to be the reason that he went back to jail, so I did what I do best. I just dealt with it.

At any rate, I made it to high school. I decided to go to the Westside Skills Center to take up a trade. I took up cosmetology. My best friend Kutana decided to do the same.

It was at this school where I met my boyfriend of eight years and my son's father, Antoine. He wanted to come to my house, but I had to tell him that my mom wouldn't allow me to have a boyfriend. I was only fifteen, and the magic age to have a boyfriend was sixteen. He went to his mother crying and confessing his love for me. She was so touched by this that she came to my house to talk to my mom.

From that point on, I was able to have a boyfriend openly. Antoine and I were close. We had a great relationship, one that other people were jealous of. We were inseparable. Neither of us had vehicles, but we went everywhere by way of JTA (Jacksonville Transportation Authority). He was even allowed to spend the night at my house even though Mom wouldn't let him sleep in our room. But come on, we were teenagers!

One night we were chilling at my mom's house.

Antoine pulled me into a room and said, "Your sister touched my nuts."

He was talking about Fhanta.

I interrogated, "What do you mean she touched your nuts?"

He said, "She just walked by me and grabbed my nuts."

This seemed too bizarre to even ask her about, but why would he lie? I mean, my sister and I got along great. Our lives and loyalty seemed to be the very opposite, and I didn't know if I could trust her.

It wasn't like if I asked her she would say, "Yes, I did. I just wanted to see what they felt like."

I was immediately reminded of Tim. I eventually asked her and as I expected, she denied it. I didn't know what to think. I trusted Antoine, but she was my sister. No matter how much she would try to compete with me, I couldn't make myself believe she would stoop so low. This was an allegation that I needed proof of in order to believe. But since there weren't any, I decided to just not deal with it. I may have had my issues, but I also had standards. You will never see me fighting over money, and you will never see me fighting over a man, especially when it comes to my family. Neither was worth the silence nor separation that came with the foolishness, so I buried the accusation.

Back in our cosmetology class, one day Antoine and I met at the lockers. We started chit chatting and being flirtatious; before you knew it, his hands were in my pants making me feel good. We were being discreet. Suddenly, out of nowhere, our friend who I'll call Will -who Kutana and I hung out with- walked by and saw what was going on. I jumped up. He told me not to worry about anything. He said he would look out. He did just that. I guess I was so far gone, because I only felt embarrassment for a quick second.

High School was the beginning of my turning point. My

teachers, Alpha Smith and Melanie Brown, really believed in me. They told me and showed me that I could do anything. Poetry was my relief and one day I shared a piece that I wrote called *"I Wanna Be Free"* with my teachers. They entered my poem into a national poetry contest. I can't remember where the contest was being held, but it was somewhere outside of Jacksonville. If I remember correctly, it was in Palatka. Both teachers along with my mom traveled there for the ceremony. It was a metaphor for what I was feeling inside mixed with what I was seeing around me. It went like this:

>From day to day, from night to night
>I sleep in darkness with shackles so tight
>Waking up in the morning, slaving hour after hour
>Master this, Master that and still can't take a shower
>No matter how hard I try, there's no way out of this disaster
>I'm tired of slaving for this so-called Master
>I don't want to feel pain, I wanna feel love, I want to be
>Oh what I would give, if I could be free.
>My children run wild and get beat with whips
>Have lumps on their lips and bruises on their hips
>No food to eat, no shelter to sleep
>Working and walking all day, not a place to soak our feet.
>I pray and pray for conditions to get better

For everyone no matter what nationality to join together
For there will be no masters over anyone, but I know
it's just a fantasy
For a chance, I wanna feel me, I wanna be free!

To my surprise, it won third place! Seeing that my teachers cared that much to invest their time and energy in me was different and made me want to be better. My grades started changing. I went from D's and F's on my report card to A's, B's, and even straight A honor roll. Things that used to bother me no longer did. Everything was going in the right direction.

My mom had a new friend named Ron Combo who became my godfather. He would take me out on different political campaigns. We would go out and canvas for different candidates. I'd spend the night at his house, and he would spoil me like I was his daughter. He has a daughter, Crystal but he treated me no different. He rented a limo for me and Antoine for Prom. Of course, I had my homies Big George, Will and my bestie Kutana with me. We had the time of our lives! And to top it off, we went to Universal Studios for Grad Nite and he paid for that. Grad Nite in itself was fun, but the ride up was a nightmare that set me back. I sat with Will on the bus, as the seat with Kutana was taken.

Antoine didn't go for whatever reason. Will was on the bus playing the song and singing, "All the things your man won't Do" by Joe on his Walkman.

I didn't think anything of it, because Will was a clown. No one took him seriously. This was why we hung out! Him and Big George kept Kutana and me laughing! I was cold, so I put my jacket over my shoulder and fell asleep.

It was about five or six o'clock in the morning as we were heading to Orlando. I woke up to his hands in my pants. I guess to him, this was his "reward" for looking out for me and Antoine that day in school. He looked at me with remorse and apologized, but the damage was done. The trust and friendship was broken. Once again, I didn't say anything. I just dealt with it, and I tried to move forward with having a good time at Grad Nite.

Then to add fuel to the fire, my godfather just disappeared out of my life. To this day, I don't know why.

The only thing I know is that he and mom had an argument, and he said, "Eff you and everyone in your family except Nikki."

Who knows what mom said after that to get under his skin?

So, it was not surprising that when we were riding the bus home from school and Kahlil asked me to fight a girl for him, I asked no questions. I had just gotten my nails done. The only thing I said was that if I broke my nail, he had to replace it. He agreed. So, there it was. He showed me my opponent. I kept quiet until we got off the bus. I walked behind her and called her name, "Amy!" She turned around. *Pow!* I stuck her and it was on. Although I came close to one or two, that was my first and only fight in high school, earning me the name of Mike Tyson from those who witnessed it.

Even though I was retained twice, I ended up graduating on time. I moved out when I was seventeen with Antoine. I went to Denise Carol modeling school afterwards, but no one showed up to support me when I graduated from there. Antoine came super late; he missed the whole event because he wanted to bring me flowers. At least that was his excuse. Mom didn't want to go because her boyfriend Marvin didn't want to, and my siblings were doing their own thing. Kahlil wanted to go, but he would have had to catch a ride with mom so that wasn't happening. However, he and my brother Charles didn't hesitate to call me to let me know how proud they were of me.

With everything I went through traumatically, holding it in became too much; I began having nightmares about it. I finally told Antoine everything. He told me to tell my mother. I put up a wall.

He said, "If you don't tell her and tell her everything, I will."

I knew it was time. Before, I had only told my mom of certain incidents. This time I knew even though I felt she wasn't going to believe me, I still had to tell her everything. I was a ticking time bomb. And so I set it up to have a conversation with her.

I can't recall how it went but I do recall mom appearing sad as she listened to me talk but her response to me felt like I wasted time once again. That spring was the Daytona Spring Break free concert. Method Man performed there, along with some other artists. He would just walk through the crowd saying, "Takow, Takow, Takow." It got the crowd hyped. I was definitely absorbed in the moment, because I was just in love with the artist at that time.

We were there with my aunt Norma, Uncle Ricky, Rochelle's cousin Reddrick and Rochelle. I don't know where Fhanta and Kahlil were. They may have gone with us, but I don't recall them being around at this moment. We were having a ball sitting down in the sand when suddenly I saw Gino walking down the strip.

It was like I felt a safety net around me, maybe because my uncle was there.

I don't know, but I yelled out, "That's the guy that raped me!"

My mom acted like she was hearing it for the first time. It definitely was my aunt's first time hearing it. Now my uncle wasn't much of a talker -at least not around me- but he smiled a lot. I guess because he knew he had the best smile. He wasn't smiling when he heard that. He jumped up and ran after him. But the perpetrator got away. I was so used to Mom brushing things off or even downplaying situations that seeing my mom act in my defense actually felt good, even if it was just in that moment. As a teenager, I knew something wasn't right about mom's actions; one minute she didn't believe me, and then the next minute she reacted to the news. I wanted to try to make sense of her behavior, because I knew she loved me. Suddenly, it hit me. My mom never talked about her past. I believed she had gone through her own trauma, and it hurt her to know that her daughter had gone through it, too. At least this is what I have told myself over the years. I made myself believe she had never dealt with hers, and that was why she couldn't deal with mine. This has gotten me through all of these years without animosity.

At that point, I was twenty years old. Antoine and I are no longer together but we share a child together. Dasjuan was about a year old. My mom had a friend named Tony.

One day my car was acting up, so mom had me reach out to Derrick, Tony's brother. He was pretty handy when something needed fixing. One day he showed up to my apartment unannounced. I guess he was seeking payment for his services or something. I don't know if he had been drinking, but he just walked in and started touching me. He pushed me towards my room.

I looked down and saw my son, Dasjuan, close to the doorway. That was all the strength and motivation I needed to finally stand up for myself with these abusers.

I implored, "You're going to rape me in front of my son?"

It stopped Derrick in his tracks. Maybe it was hearing the word *rape*, or maybe it was the fact that my son was there that made him think twice. At any rate, he left my apartment. Finally, I'd found my voice. I felt strong! I felt empowered! I felt like the next time a dirty punk decided that they wanted to put their hands on me, it would be the last time they would put their hands on anybody.

Aishia McQuillan

CHOICES & CONSEQUENCES

Growing up, I had no security or stability. The people I was supposed to trust and find comfort in let me down in one way or another. People who were supposed to be there for me always seemed to disappear.

My brother Charles used to tell me I was melodramatic, because I cried over everything. I missed my family dearly so when they visited and it was time for them to leave, I would be the only one crying. When we were wrestling and I didn't feel like continuing, I would fake being hurt just to get out of it. I didn't mind wrestling, but I had to do it often with Fhanta. She seemed to always want to challenge me. I don't think she was jealous of me; I just think we were so close in age that she wanted my spot as the oldest. I could be wrong, but I'll never know. Charles, as the older brother, had to keep us tough. Then, there was the world, that meant us no good. It just seemed like my whole life was either a fight or a struggle. After my brother called me melodramatic, I decided to build up a wall of protection. I vowed to never let anyone see me sweat again.

On the inside I was still hurting but I wouldn't allow myself to feel the pain. I released it by inflicting it on others. By no means was I this heartless soul. I was very family-oriented. I was sweet natured, and I still would do anything for anyone. I just had my ways. For instance, Kahlil used to have this high pitched voice that irked me. When we'd wrestle, that's when you'd hear it. I couldn't stand it so I would punch him in the chest every time then would tell him to put some bass in his throat. He would do it until his voice became naturally deep. He credits me for his voice being so deep.

Then, there was this one time that Kahlil and I got into an argument. I cannot remember what it was about, but the argument led into something physical. For some reason, he grew bold and thought he could beat me. So, he swung on me.

Of course, I had to dominate him. Before you know it, I had him pinned to the ground.

He was yelling, "Let me up! When I get up, I'm going to kick your butt!"

So, I let him up. I wanted to see him kick my butt. He stood there huffing and puffing.

Then he exclaimed, "I'm going to shoot myself!"

I said in the most careless tone, "Do it."

Of course, I didn't mean it. I love my brother. He and I were and still are super close. To me, this was a part of my journey of growth. Maybe it was the wrong way to handle it, but I think I knew deep down inside that he wasn't serious.

I moved out of my mom's house when I was seventeen. This wasn't too long after graduation. Mom was always fussing. This is how she got her point across to us, so I was super excited to leave her house and gain some independence of my own. Kahlil was sad to see me go, but I'll never forget what mom said to me.

She said, "The grass isn't always greener on the other side."

I was thinking *Maybe not, but it will surely be better than this place.* As kids, we think we have all the answers, and I was no different. Antoine and I moved in together into his mom's place. That was because she had just had surgery, and we wanted to look after her. Well -as sweet of a woman as she is- I quickly learned that two women cannot live under the same roof for an extended period of time. Naturally, women are emotional beings. Luckily, I knew how to control my emotions. Oftentimes, I chose not to. In this case, I would never argue with her because I had to respect her space but she was always in our business and I couldn't take it any longer. I was so frustrated with her that I wrote a poem called "Eff You, Yolander." Except the *Eff* was the real four letter word that you cannot say around your holier than thou friends. It took me a long time to feel a sense of worthiness after everything I've gone through. I wrote this for self-relief. After releasing that frustration, I was able to move forward and smile while under her roof.

I had no brain to mouth filter then. Not even to Antoine. I would talk about his mama to his face like she was a chick I had just beat down on the street. It was worse when he and I were arguing. I told him we had to go or else I was leaving by myself, and that's what we did.

We got our own place. I started going to visit my mom weekly. She lived on one side of town and I lived on another, but I was missing her. Our relationship wasn't perfect growing up, but she was all I had besides my dog Beethoven and my siblings. I made it a practice to visit Mom, because Dad instilled in me at a young age the value of family. She wasn't a bad mom at all and I only have one mom.

One weekend while I was at my mom's house, her best friend Pat happened to be there. Pat took me under her wing as a teenager. Mom decided to become a Jehovah's Witness shortly after her and Dad split. She met Pat at one of the Kingdom Halls that we attended. One day when I was thirteen, my mom gave us a choice on whether we still wanted to attend. We all chose not to.

However, Mom and Pat remained besties. Our families were

close. We would have gatherings at each other's house. Pat had two sons and two daughters. Chaka, her oldest daughter and I were close, and she still took me under her wing. She also had an older son named Dana. He didn't come around us much but often enough to be accepted into the family.

One day, we were at a gathering. As I was getting something for my mom, I found myself alone with Dana. He became a bit too flirtatious with me. His eyes said he wanted to take what wasn't his.

It was very uncomfortable and scary but he stopped himself and said, "I can't do that to you."

Whatever was on his mind, I was glad he had enough sense to control it.

I have forgiven him for the thought, and this is why he and I can communicate to this day if we need to. I never spoke of this to the family. We continued to gather as normal. I don't recall seeing Dana after that. I do recall our next gathering, though. Mom had a thing with making home movies, and at this particular time, she included Pat's children. It was me, Fhanta, Kahlil, Pat's son Walter, and her daughter Chaka. We went up the street to the nearest park and filmed a skit about a man in a dress played by Walter who robbed and killed an old sweet lady, played by Fhanta. The old lady's grandchildren, who were also thugs, sought to avenge her. They were played by me, Chaka, and Kahlil. I had so much fun doing these home movies that I decided I wanted to be an actress.

As for Pat, she was a paraprofessional. She strongly believed in education. It was high on her priority list. When it came to me, she wasn't having it. She made sure I was going to school even if she had to take me down to the college herself and force me to sign the paperwork -which she did. She was another one who believed in me with everything in her. She enrolled herself as well, and we had some of the same classes. She made it a point to be academically responsible for me. Oh, how I appreciated her for that. But when I wasn't in class, I would do stupid stuff like take things that didn't belong to me. I didn't realize it was stealing until I actually started paying attention to what I was doing. For instance, my friends would work somewhere, and they would heavily discount clothing. Luckily, we never got caught.

I would also work at a grocery store, and I'd eat from the produce section where I was working. Everyone was doing it, so it was no biggie, until I got fired for it. Ooh, I recall an incident when a girl named Katrina got caught eating produce at the same time I did. When we got called into the office and were confronted about it, she had the audacity to flip on me when we got fired.

She looked at me and said, "Oh Aishia, I have money missing out of my purse too!"

I was dumbfounded! I tried to get an understanding of what she meant while we were in the office, because we were friends!

Supposedly. We were told to take it outside. When I found out that she was actually accusing me of stealing her money, she ran into her car and rolled her windows up.

Yes, I tried my best to yank her out of the window. Our other friend grabbed me and told me she wasn't worth it. I begged to differ! I wanted her bad and vowed that no matter how long it took, vengeance was mine! She knew I hadn't taken her money. Lesson learned. Many times, people choose to be ignorant for their own convenience and think *I didn't know* is an acceptable excuse for that behavior. It was then that I learned to choose my friends carefully and that ignorance wasn't an excuse. I started paying attention to the choices I was making and stopped being careless. Because deep down inside, I knew what I was doing if I just stopped and paid attention, and maybe I wouldn't have had to deal with the accusation of being a thief.

I remember going home and telling Antoine what had happened. He was selling weed at the time and had a small group of clientele. I was so upset about what she said that I started selling for him without him knowing. I told him after I made the sell. Then I had the "fancy" idea to start pinching from the weed. He got on to me about doing that. However, when his clientele kept coming back, all of a sudden, I was a *genius*.

Somehow, I knew just the right amount to pinch without making it noticeable. Not once did I get caught. I had decided to stop when I found out I was pregnant with my firstborn. I knew then that he was the only thing that mattered, and God knew he was just what I needed to turn my life around.

I thought, *Finally! A family that can't be taken away from me.* Boy, was I wrong. What I didn't realize at the time was that the sacrifices I was making by being in school, and my after school studies were taking a toll on my relationship with Antoine. Adding a baby into the mix weighed even heavier on the relationship. A conversation came up about "watching" our son as if we were babysitters instead of parents, and Mommy mode clicked in. I went off! I told him I could raise our son by myself, and that's what I did. Six years and an engagement went down the drain just like that. Over the years, we had attempted to make it work.

We tried for two more years but love wasn't enough. I realized I had a greater purpose in my son. Even though I was mentally weak, I refused to allow anyone to see that. Everyone who knew me had always thought I was headstrong and secure when that was the opposite. It was all a façade until being headstrong was actually who I was.

I didn't take my next relationship seriously. I met Furman at Jones College where I attended. He was handsome but I was not interested initially because I had just broken it off with Antoine, but he had his eyes on me. It wasn't until this lady named Robin got jealous, because she thought we were an item, so she decided to key my car. He had no interest in her whatsoever so I -being who I was- gave her a reason to be jealous. I called my bestie up and told her what had happened.

She said, "I'm on my way."

Let's just say that by the time we finished, Robin was forking out some money to get that car back into a drivable state. We saw each other at school the next evening. She didn't say anything to me, and I didn't say anything to her. I guess she quickly realized that she had messed with the wrong one. Furman and I began officially dating. Well, because my intentions weren't good from the beginning, I ran over that whole relationship. Furman was really a great guy. He took us to Disney World. He catered to my every need. He gave me anything and everything that I wanted. He even bought me a car. Well, let's say he co-signed for the car and provided the down payment. I cared for him. I really did but he wanted to wife me.

How did I repay him? By degrading him. I would call him the worst of the worst of names. I would tell him that I could not respect him, because he acted like a female's private part; except I said that ugly word. All he wanted to do was love me, and all I wanted to do was use him.

Being a single mom was not easy. I was determined to not become a statistic. I would not be labeled as another black mother living in the ghetto. I wanted more for myself and Dasjuan. I did not have a problem visiting the ghetto as I had friends who lived there. Mom was a single mother of five and had never raised us in the 'hood, and I was determined to be the same way. I was determined not to raise my children in an impoverished environment. I made sure that my salary was always above what the average person was making. Mom taught me to keep different bank accounts and never let the right hand know what the left hand was doing. What she meant by that was have your accounts, but your man only needs to know about one. She said that this secures me if I ever had to pick up and leave. She never wanted us to be dependent on a man nor did she want us stuck in a relationship that we could not get out of. At that time I only had two accounts. When I became a single mother, those accounts became exhausted quickly as I was trying to maintain a comfortable lifestyle with Dasjuan and me. I was talking to my bestie, Kutana, about how stressful things were.

She said "Let me take you out."

I was like, "Where?"

She said, "I'm going to get us tickets to the Kings of Comedy Tour."

Steve Harvey, D.L. Hugley, Cedric the Entertainer, and Bernie Mac were coming to Jacksonville. This was huge, and I did not want to miss it.

"Heck Yeah!" I said excitedly, "Girl, we are about to wild out!"

In times like these, who couldn't use a good laugh. She and I went to the mall and bought matching outfits. I had my babysitter all set. The evening of the show, we stepped out in our long, light blue dresses. The top part of the dress was a halter top. Her long dreads were pinned up while my bra-length hair was straightened and slightly curled at the ends. Neither of us wore makeup. We both believed in our natural beauty, but we did have our lip gloss popping. We were excited to be at the show. We laughed so hard at all of the comedians. After the show, we were walking to my car and saw the limo that the entertainers were in. We walked by it, and the bodyguard asked us if we wanted to go in.

We looked at each other and said, "Yes!"

We got in, and one of the comedians asked us to come sit next to him. I won't say his name, because I found out later that he was married and still is. We will just call him Blue. We talked and laughed. Blue then invited us back to their hotel. They were going to take us in their limo.

Kutana and I discussed going then I told her, "We're not going anywhere without our own transportation."

I never liked to be put in a situation where I was not in control. If we needed to leave, I wanted to make sure we had the means to. We knew what was on his mind, but we wanted to go with him just for the clout. Before we got out of the limo, he made sure we were going to meet him. We followed the directions to the room where he was staying. He let us in, and we laughed and talked some more. It felt like we were friends, but I knew what it was. After some time went by, Blue proposed a threesome with us. I was not down with that. Even though I don't think Kutana wanted the ménage à trois, she did want to have sex with him just for the experience. They talked about having sex without me since I wasn't with it. I wanted to go. Blue told her to let me leave, and he would take her home in his limo.

"Absolutely not," I asserted, "We came together, we leave together."

Kutana and I talked about this a little more, as she really wanted to stay. But I was not letting up.

Blue then said, "Well, I'm going to go take a shower and let y'all talk."

He left and went into the bathroom.

"Let's rob him," Kutana proposed.

I pondered it but said, "Nah, let's just go."

"We're just going to leave like that, like before he gets out of the shower?"

I responded with "Yep, and guess what? He will forget all these women that he sleeps with from city to city, but he'll always remember the two that left his balls blue."

We laughed as we walked down the hallway discussing what his face might have looked like when he walked out the bathroom and saw us gone.

"I bet he thought we were going to join him in the shower," I chuckled.

We laughed some more. What I found out in later

conversation was, as we were talking and laughing, she was trying to find a way to ditch me so that she could get back to Blue. There were a lot of celebrities in the hotel that night. One person was Pleasure P from a group called Pretty Ricky. We walked by an open door; I peeked inside from the hallway, because it was popping with music and dim lights.

Somebody yelled out, "If you ain't eating Cooter cat [except he used the vulgar word] then get out!"

We scurried up out of there. What a night! It definitely took my mind off of the bills.

A few months after this event, things were not looking better. My electricity was about to get cut off. I called my bestie again and told her that I was thinking about dancing at the strip club for a while. She told me that she was not going to let me do it alone. I was embarrassed by the thought, so we went across town to strip. We did not want anyone to see us. We walked in during the daytime. The owner was telling us how beautiful we looked and how we would be a great fit there. Then he pulled out an application. I did not know we had to fill out applications to be strippers!

I grabbed the clipboard then looked at Kutana and said, "I can't do this," then we walked out.

She was happy because she didn't really want to do it either, but she was my rider. Whatever we did -good or bad- we were doing it together.

I then dated a guy from Maryland. He and I would write steamy poetry to each other. When he would visit, we would bring those writings to life. One time, he came to Jacksonville for a visit. He tried to teach me how to drive a stick shift right in the middle of Orange Park. Anyone from the Jacksonville/Orange Park area knows that you're playing Russian roulette, because that is a high traffic area. I was so scared. I panicked too much behind the wheel and made him take over. I never learned how to drive a stick shift but, that day he drove us to the Orange Park mall. He stopped at a jewelry store, bought me an engagement ring, and proposed. I was so embarrassed! I couldn't show it, because I didn't want to embarrass him. So, I did what any sweet and innocent person with a heart would do: I said yes. He was good enough to screw, because buddy was touching every inch of my body just right. But to marry? I just couldn't see myself waking up next to him every day. I mean he was nice and sweet, but I am not the marriage type, at least not then. I wanted to play. We were at the store and everyone was clapping and congratulating us on our "engagement," and I had just made him the happiest man in the world.

Great. Somebody pass me a shot of the strongest liquor you have and when you find something stronger, give me a shot of that too, I thought. All wasn't lost though.

I could just use this as an opportunity to get up north closer to my dad in Philadelphia, I thought. I went home and told my mom that I had just gotten engaged and that I was moving to Maryland. My mom asked me if I loved him. I told her yes, and so she said I had her blessing. I remember Kahlil crying and hugging me tight.

When I got to Maryland, I found out that Mr. Maryland had daughters. This was something he neglected to tell me. It really didn't bother me, but I used it as an excuse for why the relationship wasn't going to work out. Within two weeks, I was out of there!

I made it up to Delaware where I visited my uncle Tony and aunt Reba for a few days; then I found out I was pregnant. I wanted to be closer to my mom during the pregnancy, so I drove all the way back home. The plan failed. I never even made it to Philly. Dasjuan was just an infant when we were traveling back. We had made it to South Carolina when suddenly, I was disturbed by blue and red lights. I was scared! Not because I was speeding. I was used to that. I was terrified because I was going ninety miles per hour. I could have gone to jail in an unknown state for reckless driving. My son could have been taken away from me for child endangerment! I just wanted to make it home. All I know is it was nothing but the grace of God that the cop who pulled me over turned around and left me there. He must have gotten an emergency call or something, but I thank God I was no longer a priority.

I did the speed limit all the way through Georgia. I must confess, I did pick it back up once I hit the Florida state lines.

But I only went like ten miles over the limit. This was the way I would do things. I was living life in the fast lane, and I was proud to fancy myself after being with my father's child. After a few weeks, I miscarried. I was not upset at all. As a matter of fact, I was relieved. I was about twenty one years old, and I was not trying to have different babies by different men. I was not in the headspace to be in a committed relationship. To be clear, I did not sleep with every man I dated, and I always presented myself as a lady. At the same time, if we had a sexual connection, who was I to stand in the way? I got what I wanted until I did not want it anymore. Truth be told, I got bored with men easily. This is why I never saw myself as marriage material, but most guys that I dated did. A few even tried to put a ring on it. I knew that they were only falling in love with what they saw, not all of me. I joke and say that I keep the other side of me locked up in a vault. That person can be mean, heartless, reckless, and will fight in a heartbeat. Most people did not see that side of me but enough did to vouch for her existence.

This is not to suggest that I didn't care for people along the way, because I did. For instance, there was this one guy that I messed around with. He was a model. His body was cut in all the right places. He was just gorgeous. His name was Kevin. We met at work. He didn't work at the company where I did, but he modeled for them. We locked eyes, and it was on. After our first rendezvous, I was sprung and had him sprung too. The sex was super hot. I mean "breaking beds hot," "sex on the countertops hot," "any and every position hot!" But neither of us was ready to take it to the next level.

It was more than just sex with us though. We had an unspoken connection. One that neither of us was ready to admit. One birthday night, I was in the club with my girls, Raffelle and Arnitra. Rafelle's friend, Shay, joined us along with another girl. I don't remember her name. I just remember her being tall, white, and I think she had long, brown hair. She was super cool, but I only met her that night and never saw her again after that. Everyone had money to get in except me. Raffelle told me that she would pay my way in because it was my birthday, so we ended up in the V.I.P section. I started dancing and shaking my tail feathers. The next thing you know, dollars were being thrown at me. I wasn't stripping. I was just dancing and winding my body to the music with my clothes on.

When the song went off, I counted the money and what do you know, I had one hundred dollars! I paid Raffelle back. I thought, *Dang, happy birthday to me!* Shortly after, I saw Kevin. He obviously had just gotten into an altercation with someone and his friends were trying to calm him down. He wasn't trying to hear it. We locked eyes, and he immediately calmed down. No words were exchanged, just looks. I guess some relationships just aren't meant to be broken. To date, we are good friends -nothing more, nothing less.

During this time, I decided to focus on myself. I thought about how mom would have us acting in those home movies and decided I wanted to give acting a try. I sought out different acting agencies. I was accepted at John Casablancas Models & Talent. I learned what I needed to, and then I got the call. Not from the modeling agency but from Fhanta.

"Nik, I have a gig for you. I know this guy who is filming this movie. He wanted me to be in it, but I told him I wasn't interested. However, my sister is looking to break into the industry."

I couldn't believe what I was hearing! My sister came through. She gave me the info. Immediately, when we got off the phone, I made the call.

"Hello, Chad. This is Aishia, Fhanta's sister..."

He gave me the rundown of a movie that he was filming called *Two Heads, One Brain* from Two Crackers and a Lamp Production.

I was skeptical at first until he said, "It's not a porno."

He told me that it was about a guy who continuously allowed his little head to lead his life instead of his big head. As long as I didn't have to take my clothes off, I was in. So, we shot the movie. I realized I was born to do this. So, I continued to seek out other opportunities.

After that film, I didn't have to audition for anything locally because I was booking jobs by word of mouth from others. I ended up being in a stage play called *City of Passions*.

The work started flowing in. I was then in an Independent Film called *After the Buzzard Sounds*. That one was really fun to film. After production was over, we had a red carpet event with the comedian Pierre Edwards hosting it. Mom started to take notice that I was serious about acting as a career and began to travel with me. She would even drive down to Miami with me just for an audition and then drive back. That drive was crazy. My hair was already down my back, but Mom wanted me to try wearing a wig that day. It's just something with her and wigs. If you have a head, she's going to try to stick one on you. I didn't make it three miles up the road before I yanked that thing off my head. My scalp was sweating and itching. It just wasn't for me. Luckily, I had a comb and brush in the car. I remember Mom telling me as we were traveling that out of all of my siblings, I'm the one who contacts her and checks up on her the most. I told her not to worry about that; everyone just gets caught up in their own lives, but I only have one Mom. I said my siblings will soon realize that, too.

This was the turning point in our relationship. She and I became closer. We began to talk on the phone almost every day. As a teenager, I thought my mom only loved me out of obligation, because it seemed like she never listened to me. She was always fussing at me, and I didn't feel like she had my back when it came to others hurting me. But mom started showing interest in me and the things I liked to do. I began to talk to her about my relationships.

When she heard something she didn't like, she'd say, "I'll knock him out!"

Mom started being protective over me, and it was very much appreciated.

I managed to book several other jobs ranging from local music videos, independent films, and movie shorts. I was even an uncredited actress in the movie *Sydney White* starring Amanda Bynes. My favorite gig was when I played Skye in a book trailer for the talented novelist, Brenda Jackson. It was for her book, *Slow Burn*.

Life was just going great. I found my passion in acting, and I was going to stop at nothing to pursue it. I have a homegirl named Valerie. We met on the set of *County Road 14* directed by MysterE Visions. She and I have been in a few other movies as well which is how we became friends. She seemed to always have the celebrity hook up. One day she and I went to a club at the Jacksonville Landing and met with RZA from the Wu-Tang Clan. I don't recall how they met, but I do remember us going to sit in the V.I.P. section where he was. We sipped on a couple of drinks, danced a little, and hung out with him until the club closed for the night. He was super cool! He invited her to go with him to watch a Rugby game that very next day. She asked me to go with her which I did and really, I had no idea rugby could be so interesting! I thought we were going to network to break into the industry, but we were having so much fun at the game that we just enjoyed the moment.

My life was starting to change. People in my local community were starting to notice me from different movies I had been in. They were asking for my autograph on multiple occasions. I had been around a few celebrities, and I just started to feel that I was on the right path. My attitude toward people started changing for the better. I began to have a filter; I knew that in the acting field, I could not present myself as a difficult person to work with. I've always been sweet; there was just that mean streak I had that needed reconstruction. Once again, I started working on myself. At this time, I was working at Bombardier Capital, collecting on first party financial loans. I went back to work and was talking about my accomplishments to my friends, Marvia and Dennis. I told them about the movie I was in, *2 Heads 1 Brain*; of course, they were happy for me. The next thing I know, I got called into Human Resources. This guy named Walter -who had made a few minor advances at me that I turned down- had gone to HR on me. He was "offended" by the title of the movie that I was in. Not only was Walter a bit chubby and unattractive in my eyes, but his fiance worked in the same company, same department and sat only a few seats away from us. *The audacity,* I thought. The HR Personnel's name was Tammy Hatfield.

I said, "Tammy, I was just talking about the movie I was in."

She said, "I understand, but because he got offended, we have to fire you for sexual harassment."

I was in disbelief! She did apologize and I could tell that she did not want to do it. That day, I learned just how pervasive sexual harassment in the workplace was. I was embarrassed to even have that on my record. If anyone should've been fired for sexual harassment, it should have been him. I guess because I turned down his advances, I was a threat and he had to eliminate the threat. This was the first test to my growth, I guess because a part of me wanted to tell his fiance and everyone else about how he had been flirting with me but I decided it wasn't worth it. I received a phone call later that day saying that it was like a revolt at Bombardier that day I got fired. That made me feel a little better that people were supporting me. But I thought, *how in the world will I get another job with a sexual harassment on my record?*

One day after I came back from job searching, I saw a friend of Furman, the guy I dated in college. I asked about him, and what I was told next broke my heart. My ex's friend told me that Furman had a brain aneurysm, and it was because of the foolishness I put him through. I understand that I was young at the time, but I should have never disrespected him the way that I did. He did nothing but love me. I felt super guilty. That was confirmation that it was time for me to grow up. I mean, I was a huge Brian McKnight fan. So huge that I would often have crazy fantasies about us. Furman drove me to Orlando's House of Blues to see him perform, knowing how I felt about him. If it weren't for him taking me there, I would have never met him. This man would do anything for me. I needed to find Furman somehow and apologize, but I didn't know how to get in touch with him. I knew that no matter how long it took, I would tell him I was sorry for how I treated him when we were together. Eventually, Facebook came along, and I was able to locate him. I apologized as I said I would. He accepted and told me that he understood that I was young. Talk about a weight lifted!

After I found out about what I did to Furman, I decided to open my heart to a dedicated, respectful, monogamous relationship. I met a guy named Cedric. Cedric was fine! He was light-skinned, tall, and slender. He reminded me of a younger Boris Kodjoe. He was churchgoing. He would have made someone a great husband one day. I really liked him, but Cedric was abstinent. We would fool around but my kitty refused to pause, it kept purring! It was like dangling Fancy Feast in front of a cat but not letting it have it. He then took me to his church, Shiloh. I don't remember the word preached, but I remember the feeling. It was the first church that I went to since leaving the Jehovah's Witness congregation. It was nothing like the Witnesses made it out to be. The Preacher was calm, the teaching was bible-based, when the choir started singing, there was this indescribable presence in the atmosphere. I did not like when the Pastor asked for all visitors to stand so that we could be acknowledged. I hate being put on the spot. Furthermore, I don't like a lot of attention being placed on me, especially if I'm not seeking it. However, I did enjoy myself. *I could get used to this*, I thought. But I still was not completely ready. I thought we had to be perfect to be in church, even though Cedric told me it was "come as you are." It still did not register. Cedric seemed perfect; the Jehovah's Witnesses seemed perfect; and me, I was not ready to give up my imperfect lifestyle. I was having fun. I wanted to change certain things about me but not everything about me.

I really did try to abstain from sex for Cedric, and it felt good that I was trying. Nonetheless, my body was yearning, and eventually, my eyes started wandering. I then met this guy while still dating Cedric. His name is Jamal. He lived in my apartment complex. He was tall and slender built. He had a nice brown complexion with a goatee. He also had pretty teeth. Those features combined were a dangerous combination for me. He also dressed like a northerner. I found out later that he was from New Jersey. He and I talked a couple of times. Conversations were interesting. One day he just popped up at my apartment while Cedric was there. For the first time ever, I got caught. Jamal and I weren't sleeping together then, but the attraction was there.

I will never forget the dispirited look on Cedric's face. I pretended to not be bothered, but it affected me a bit. Cedric fell off the face of the earth. To this day, there isn't one trace of him. I continued to see Jamal. He was super intelligent. I enjoyed our conversations more than anything.

I ended up finding employment at CitiStreet as a Benefits Specialist. I drove a gold Suzuki Grand Vitara. I loved that SUV. As a matter of fact, it was my first and last SUV. I remember lending it to Kahlil so that he could take his son, Hymea back to his mother's house. This was before my brother got custody of him. I told him to take Hymea home and bring my car right back, because I had to go to work the next morning. I fell asleep for the night. I woke up to Tot's phone call.

She uttered in a panic, "Nikki, Kahlil called me because he was scared to call you. He wrecked your car."

"What!" I yelled, "What the eff you mean he wrecked my car? I'm going to beat his butt!"

I meant that. My mouth was filthy like a sailor. It was raining hard the next morning, and the car hydroplaned. I can't remember if he hit another vehicle or if he hit the median. I was so upset that I don't even remember how I got on the scene. All I know is that my brother was in the back of the police car. I told him that if the police weren't there then I would wail out on his butt. The police said that he would turn his head. He ended up totaling my car. Anytime he asked me to use my car after that, I'd remind him of my Grand Vitara.

I would get Jamal to take me to work and pick me up until I got another car. About a year into the relationship, he and I moved in together. It was more by force, because things just started falling apart financially. I was getting evicted from my apartment. After we moved in together I noticed a big change in him. He started to become possessive and jealous. I will never forget when he thought I was cheating on him. He had no reason to think that. It was all in his head. I found out later that it was because he was cheating on me. When he questioned me, he made me feel like I was in an interrogation room! Every time I think about that day, it reminds me of the intensity in the scene on *Menace to Society* when Bill Duke had Tyrin Turner (Kane) in the interrogation room.

He said, "You know you done effed up right."

I was totally innocent! He had a way of turning everything around on me and making me feel guilty, even when he was in the wrong. But here's the thing: he waited until we moved in together to show that side of him.

What was I to do? I was already head over heels in love with him. I put up with his cheating, lying, and mental abuse. Things became so bad that I started watching *Investigation Discovery* to see what criminals were doing to murder people and how they got caught, so that I wouldn't make the same mistakes.

Then, I got pregnant. That was a time when I was supposed to be happy and glowing. Two months in, I was walking in our apartment complex taking Dasjuan to the park. Jamal was driving home. He didn't realize he was passing me because he was so focused on the female walking past the dumpster with shorts that cut into her butt. He turned his head almost like the exorcist to see her. If I was in the street, he would have hit me. It was at that moment that I decided not to keep the baby.

By this time, I was twenty three and did not want to be stuck in a baby momma/baby daddy relationship with this guy for eighteen years, going through pure hell the whole time. I knew it was not the baby's fault; that was my mistake. I knew it was not fair to the baby, and I asked God to forgive me for a long time afterwards. I did not want to be a single mother raising two children on my own; one was hard enough. I've never been one to depend on a man anyway. I consulted with my mom first.

She said "Nidda, you made your bed, you gotta lay in it."

Yes, I put myself in this situation, but it did not feel good. I had to make a decision, and regretfully, I stuck to it. He made me feel so guilty when I told him what I did. He told me that it was probably Antoine's baby anyway. That hurt, because at this point, I had not cheated on him. He made me feel so bad about the abortion by bringing it up every chance he got that I allowed myself to get pregnant from him again. I allowed this man to take me to my lowest point ever in life.

I recall a time when I was getting up with my girls, Raffelle and Arnitra. We met up at the Regency Mall back when it was popping. I had no idea that Jamal and his homies were there, too. In the course of our relationship, he made it a point to not tell me where he was going. He ended up seeing me before I saw him. He came up to me as I was walking and confronted me loudly and with all ignorance in the mall. He asked me what I was doing there and told me that I needed to take my butt home. It was so embarrassing! I did not clap back, because I just wanted that moment to go away as quickly as possible. I don't like a lot of attention on me, especially when it's negative. I decided to stay classy and pay him no attention. My girls were speechless! They could not believe he had just done that to me.

This guy I didn't know came up to me and asked me if I was okay. He was ready to put his hands on Jamal for disrespecting me, but I told him he was just being stupid and convinced him I was alright.

I literally felt like this was my karma for all of the wrong that I did to the guys in my past. I thought I was supposed to take this abuse. I also knew that I wasn't innocent either, so I decided to stay with him and go to counseling.

I wanted him to go, but he refused. So, I did it for myself. I found out that my lack of respect for men was due to my past. Until I confronted that, I would never be able to move forward. The counselor was right but I did not know how to confront my past. I did the only thing I knew to do this whole time: work on me. I was also told that this was the reason why my sexual appetite was so high and unusual. I confided in my counselor and told her something I'd never told a single soul. I'd been too embarrassed to speak about it until now. I disclosed that I had relations with a woman. My sexual appetite was like a drug. You started off with weed and then want something stronger, something more satisfying. But you never reached that level. That's where I was with sex.

The difference was, it was all in my head. For instance, I could fantasize about having multiple partners, but I had too much self-respect to see it through. But the thought would take me to a climax like never before. The same with being with another woman. The thought of two women would turn me on but I never had the desire to put it into action.

One day an opportunity presented itself, and I reluctantly decided to take it. I was nervous, but I tried not to let it show.

We got started, then she said, "You've never done this before, have you?"

I said, "No."

She said it was obvious as she chuckled. It was weird. It was nothing like my fantasy, nor did it do anything for me. That was when I realized it was just the obsession that did it for me. I guess I was confused and trying to find myself. That was something that I prayed to go away. Surprisingly, it did instantly.

The counselor told me that this may be because I'd never confronted my past. So, that's what I did. I decided to start with the easiest part first, me. I wasn't taking anymore "Karma." I was going to get back to loving myself.

Here comes the test. One day after this, a text message came across Jamal's phone. It was a woman talking about them hooking up. I didn't confront him then. I waited until he left for work. He worked the 7:00 p.m. to 3:00 a.m. shift that night. I called Antoine since I knew Jamal was jealous of him. I told him I wanted to hook up.

That's exactly what we did. I came back home and wrote a long note explaining that I knew that he'd been cheating, and that I had been putting up with it like a dummy. I reminded him that I wasn't ugly, and I could have any man that I wanted. I said that cheating is a choice, and I had chosen not to cheat up until now. I told him that I cheated that night so now he can see how I have been feeling. I put it into his sock drawer, because it was customary for him to come in and shower after work. Then I slept naked.

He couldn't get upset. He told me he saw me naked and thought he was going to get some but couldn't after reading that note. It was like I had his attention for about a month. It seems as if he was more attentive to me. He was home more instead of hanging out with his friends. But in no time, he was back to his old ways. He received a phone call from an unknown number. I looked at the phone and then saved the number in my phone. I never had the courage to call the number until one day I was going through my phone, and I mistakenly hit it. I hung up really fast.

The caller called me back. I told her I didn't mean to call her. She said, "Oh, you're Jamal's girlfriend. I've been sleeping with Jamal. I will tell you everything."

I was curious as to how she even knew who I was. Apparently, she had been going through his phone and had my number as well. I didn't even ask because it didn't matter. What mattered was that she said she recognized me as the girlfriend, she was sleeping with my man, and there was more to tell. At this point, I couldn't run from it. I listened and then confronted Jamal. He didn't deny it. I argued, cried, and swung on him. I was in pain. I wasn't hitting him hard at all. I just needed to release some tension.

He said, "You'd better stop hitting me before I hit you back."

I didn't care. I had four years of oppression to release. The more he talked, the more I wanted to fight, but he would never hit me.

He justified his cheating by saying, "She is a nobody" and "Are you really gonna let her break us up, like really?"

It was at that moment when I realized I was better than everything I had subjected myself to. I told him it was over. I attempted to lock him out of the house, but he called the cops. Because both of our names were on the condo, I had to let him back in.

He tried to get me arrested by telling the officer I was beating on him.

The officers replied, "Do you expect me to believe that she, as small as she is, was beating on you?"

He said, "Yes!"

One of the officers told him that he didn't believe him.

I told them I would rather leave. They were more concerned about mine and the kids' safety than his. I couldn't believe he tried to have me arrested. It also helped that my demeanor was calm when they came, and he was still a bit irate.

Nevertheless, I left and never looked back. I didn't want to move back home. After all, I was grown with two kids. Mom and I were getting along so well without me being under her roof, and I wanted it to stay that way. So, I called Tot up and asked if I could stay with her for a few days. My boss at the time knew what I was going through and offered to let me stay in his apartment. He said he wouldn't be there, and he would stay with his girlfriend until I got back on my feet. I was so touched that I took him up on his offer. His girlfriend was cool with that, too. She and I were cool with each other from her coming up to the Agency where I worked.

One day he said that he needed to come back to stay at his apartment but I didn't have to leave. *Nope!* I thought. I'd been through too much to trust this situation, so I picked up immediately and left. I stayed the night at a female friend's house and then sucked it up. I made the call.

"Mom, I need to come home for a while until a place comes through for me."

And of course her doors are always open.

The crazy thing about this was, when I walked away from the relationship, all kinds of doors started opening for me.

It was like God was showing me the blessings that I was blocking by holding onto this toxic relationship. The funny thing is, I wasn't a Christian but I immediately recognized the favor and the power that came from my decision. Don't get me wrong, I still loved him and still wanted to be with him. But I knew being with him was dangerous to my self-esteem and what I was trying to accomplish. Honestly, I yearned to be with this man for a long time even after I left him. I'd often listen to Brian McKnight. His music was soothing to my soul. One night, his song *One Last Cry* came on. I thought about Jamal. I heard this song a million times before. As a matter of fact, it was one of my favorites because Brian McKnight sings it with such passion. This time, I loved it for a different reason. Finally, I decided not to shed any more tears over him. No matter what, I was not going back.

My need for peace was much bigger than my desire for him. It took six years to get him completely out of my system.

On the road to recovery, I decided I wanted to take a break. That relationship was exhausting. By this time, my mom and I had repaired our relationship. We were closer than ever. As a matter of fact, we were closer than any of my other siblings were to her. She was like my best friend now. I went to her house to check on her. She was about to go to the store because she was out of Crown Royal, her favorite drink. I told her I would ride with her.

At the liquor store she would go up to random people and say, "My daughter is single!"

I was like, "Mom!"

She would crack up. I would tell her on multiple occasions "I am single for a reason. And anyway, the last place that I want to find someone is in a liquor store. I guess you want your son in law to be an alcoholic, huh?"

I'd continue. She'd think it was so funny. I enjoyed being single. The next day, she and her best friend Dot told me they had someone they wanted me to meet.

Oh no! There was no way I would let these two single women hook me up. I was certain there was a reason why these two women were single. Mom insisted he was fine. She told me it was Dot's nephew, Tye, so I finally agreed to meet. We met at Dot's daughter, Shonti's house. When I walked in the door I was greeted by two handsome men. One was my cousin Jermaine, Shonti's husband.

But the other one was like whoa! He was tall, like a football player, with a caramel crème complexion, and hazel eyes. His teeth were just perfect and his smile was infectious. Brother was fine! Mom introduced us and we hit it off immediately. We exchanged numbers and kept in contact. He was what I was missing in my life. He was the male version of me. The only problem was he didn't live locally. He lived in North Carolina.

How could I trust him; there was no way I could get serious with him. I decided I would make him my toy.

Every time he would come to visit, either he would have a girlfriend or I would have a boyfriend, but it never stopped us from flirting with each other. We both knew deep down inside that we belonged together. One day my cell phone was about to get cut off. He told me he was going to pay the bill. He never did and the phone was disconnected. It was then that I decided that I didn't want to mess with him anymore. Even though my phone was cut back on shortly after, my number was changed, and I let that be the reason for not contacting him again. I really enjoyed being single. I really just wanted to get back to my acting career and focus on creating a better life for me and my children.

Aishia McQuillan

THE WRONG HANDS

I've always been a protector. If someone wanted to harm me, I chose whether or not I wanted to defend myself. Most times I did but when someone wanted to harm my family, there was only one option, retaliate! Some will look at this as a good thing but I'm not too sure, because when it came to family, I had a different mindset. I was ready and willing to go to jail at any cost. I recall this one incident where my sister Tot called me and told me that her daughter's dad was beating on her. I told her that I would be right over. When I got there, I went straight into the kitchen. He just so happened to call and threaten her again.

I heard her say "No, don't come over here."

I yelled out "Nah! Tell him to come on!"

I had boiled some grits as soon as I got there and was going to douse him right when he stepped foot through the door. I don't know if God was saving him, me, or the both of us. I do know that sometimes I need protection from myself. All I know is, in retrospect, I'm glad he did not come that day because I'd probably still be doing time now.

I don't have time for foolishness which is why I was enjoying the single life. It had been over a year since I dated. I was a big flirt so of course I had my fun but I was having more fun with my children. My acting career was taking off, I had no male drama and life felt so good. Even though I didn't have a desire to be in a relationship, it happened anyway, with this guy, A.H

I'm only using his initials because some names are just not meant to be repeated. Nevertheless, he was super skinny, made of nothing but bones and brown flesh. He had long dreads that complimented his slender face. We met at work when I was working at a collection agency called Enhanced Recovery Company (ERC). I had no physical attraction to him but he kept me laughing. He hung tight with me and my homegirl Trina Hannah. She was short, beautiful and skinny. She dressed really cute. She loved wearing Asian outfits. They complimented her Asian eyes and round face. Of the many things she and I have in common, music is one of them. She constantly made CD's for me with the best music mix. I mean, we talked about everything.

When I say everything, I mean…everything! She is one of few people who I can say are loyal and will keep it one hundred with me.

At work, Trina, A.H., and I were basically a trio. He was good for entertainment. He wasn't comedian funny but he was stupid funny. One day after work, he and I were talking; we found out that our mothers were friends who used to work together in the mortgage industry. I immediately called my mom afterwards to get more information. She told me their family members were good people. She also said that Roxanne, A.H's mother, had some handsome boys.

Following that was, "I know he is going to treat you well, Nidda, because she didn't play with those boys."

Nidda was a special name that my mom gave me in my older years. It is special because she gave me this name after we became almost like besties. Everyone called me by my many nicknames but Mom is the only one who calls me Nidda. It was like she made herself known to the world that she stood above the rest, and I accepted it in all honor.

Anyway, A.H. let me know he was interested in dating me. The only problem was that he had a daughter whose life he wasn't in. I told him there was no way he could be in my life and not in his daughter's. I had kids myself so that was very important to me. He promised to start seeing his daughter, which he did. It was at that point that we started dating. He was so loving and attentive to my needs. I'll never forget one of the rare times that I got sick; I caught Pneumonia. After a few days of me missing work, he took a few days off of work to take care of me. Everyone knew how tight we were at the job, even the general managers. So when he requested that time off to attend to me, it was no problem with them.

More days passed and I still couldn't break my fever. It seemed like we had tried everything. We tried different medicines like Ibuprofen and Tylenol, but neither worked. We placed a cold rag over my head, and it did not work. These things were only a temporary fix but the fever came back.

One day, A.H, said, "Forget this!"

I had no idea what he was talking about. Apparently sex had been on homeboy's mind for days because he grabbed my legs and spreaded them east and west. He then placed his head between them and went to work! I mean, the anatomy was amazing! I literally felt the fever leaving my body instantly. If a couple is married, and the male has fallen ill, I will advise the female to give head! That mess works! I am living proof!

Anyway, months later, it was time for me to renew my lease, and A.H. asked me to move in with him. He lived in a house his mother owned. It was off forty sixth street on the east side of Jacksonville. I hesitated but then agreed. Together, we packed everything with the help of my two boys, Dasjuan and Jabari. We cleaned my apartment and headed to our new home.

I knew I had made a mistake when we pulled up, and he showed me off to his cousin C as if I was some type of prized possession. He came to me and squeezed my butt with two hands as if he was showing it off to his cousin. We had been dating for over a year at this time but I felt like we had just met at a club. I was upset, but I didn't say anything at that moment because I was in his territory. I needed to feel my way first since I had my boys to think about.

He asked me in a joking manner if I wanted to be a prostitute, and work for his cousin. I excused it, but in my mind, I was furious.

He didn't push the issue. He knew better. He was a bit nervous about asking. You could tell there was some type of pressure there. If only he knew he was one call away from being dealt with for asking me that, he would have kept his mouth quiet. At that point in my life, I had an army of people ready to protect me. I was looked at as "sister" to a lot of males that I came in contact with over the years, including my own biological brothers. This wouldn't have gone down pretty had I told anyone. They were so lucky that I respected A.H.'s mother. These wannabes had no idea about the game. I could probably school them on a thing or two. You're supposed to go after those whose mind you can control, not just anybody. If I didn't have kids, I probably would have infiltrated their whole operation and then took them down. I knew I had to move to plan B quickly, which was to find another apartment for me and my children.

A.H. would stay out late at night, and I really didn't care. My mind was already set. My focus was on me and my boys. He would always find little things to argue about, but then he would do things like take my phone or laptop and hide them afterwards. A.H. had a daughter that I took on as my own. Her name was Tiana. I loved that girl so much! She was my daughter, and I was her Momma IshBoo. She called me Momma Ishboo because her dad called me Ish (pronounced Eesh). That's what a lot of people call me for short instead of saying Aishia.

When A.H. and I would argue, I'd grab Tiana and my boys and we'd find some place to ride out to and have fun. I'd take them to the park, the pool, to get ice cream, or we'd go out to eat. We even went to my mom's one day and chilled over there for a while; she and I painted our nails and got into Mom's pool. I never told A.H where we were going because I didn't want him to come at me with foolishness. One thing I can say is that he never had a problem with me getting her.

His petty got to the point where he would take my car keys so I wouldn't go anywhere. This was exhausting! In the meantime I was still applying for apartments. One time, he used my cucumber melon body wash. I was livid! I started thinking he was a homosexual. When I confronted him about it, he said, "I like the smell."

Oh no, Joker! This is not normal, I thought.

He came out of the bathroom, and we started arguing. He grabbed me, and we wrestled. I swear I had a thought to grab the lamp shade and bust him upside the head with it, but all I could do was think of my boys in the back room. I didn't want to alert them. He had me pinned but only because I was fighting in silence, I guess you could say, for my kids' sake. They were protective over me. Had I put my strength on him, I seriously could have overtaken him. One thing about me, I have never dated a guy who I thought I couldn't physically take.

I remember thinking, *This dude is so weak. If someone tried to harm us, I'd be the one protecting this family, geesh!* Dasjuan and Jabari ended up hearing something so they came to check on me. We pretended to be playing when they came in. It was easy to pretend because it wasn't much of a scuffle.

Anyway, he left the house, and I started planning our summer trip to Philadelphia. He talked about going with me but he was nowhere close to being worthy of meeting my family.

Later that night, I took a shower. I then said a quick prayer and asked God to come through for us with an apartment. The shower is my sanctuary. That's where I go to find peace and gather my thoughts. So, as the suds were running down my body, I became overwhelmed with emotion. I started thinking about my boys and how I had to pretend only to protect them. I also thought about some of the decisions I have been making, like not renewing my lease to go and stay with someone else. Mom taught me better than that. She always told me to make sure that I had my own. She had always told me that if I moved in with someone, make sure my name was on the lease and always keep a separate bank account.

I never shared an account with anyone, but I put myself and my children in a bad situation.

Before you knew it I said in a desperate outcry, "Lord, I need you!"

I literally got frustrated with God, because I felt I had made several attempts previously to get near him and they all failed. I didn't think he was listening to me. Afterall, why would he? I had done so much bad to people.

I continued to release my frustration, "You know what it is going to take to get me to you! Why don't you show me what it is?" I ended with telling God I wasn't strong enough to do this on my own. I leaned my weak body against the shower wall and let the water run down my body before sitting down on its floor. Hot water ran over me some more until it turned cool. The coolness of the water gave me enough energy to get out. I remember after that just laying on the bed in my nakedness with the doors locked. I was physically, mentally, and spiritually drained.

About a month later, Mom called me up and told me she was throwing a surprise birthday party for Dot's fiftieth birthday. She said it was going to be in North Carolina, which was where

Dot was from. She was renting a mansion, and she wanted me to come. I was ecstatic! The last time I had been to North Carolina was with Furman for my family reunion fifteen years ago. I was ready!

    A.H. asked if he could go. I told him no. If I remember correctly, Bill, a friend of Mom and Dot's, needed a ride up there so my Mom asked if I could bring him. I had never met him before the night that we traveled, but I trusted that my mom would not put me in harm's way. I initially sat leaning close to the door, ready to jump out of the car if necessary. But I quickly realized I had nothing to worry about with Bill. He was one of the coolest guys you would ever meet. My sister, Tot, had watched my boys for me that weekend so I didn't have to worry about them.

 I had just gotten paid when we left that Friday which was perfect timing. Bill took care of the first gas fill up. When we got to the halfway point, I told him I had it. I used my debit card at the pump, and he pumped the gas.

    I was thinking about my next moves in life when it was interrupted by a knock on the window.

    "Ms. Nikki. Um, your card only stopped at fifty cents."

    "What!"

    I was dumbfounded! I had just gotten paid, but it was slow in hitting my account for some reason, so all that he was able to pump was the fifty cents that I had in my account. Of course that was getting us nowhere. Bill came through though. He filled us up, and we kept going. Of course he had to rag on me the rest of the trip about those fifty cents.

We finally made it to North Carolina. We were exhausted as it was late at night. We met up with my mother at this three story mansion on the beach the next night. I helped her with last minute decorations and waited for the party to start. I walked from the kitchen to the living room area that was on the second floor. I noticed this tall, handsome, light-skinned, hazel-eyed guy, Tye, standing in the walkway with a cup in his hands. This was the same guy I met in Jacksonville at my cousins Shonti and Jermaine's house. He had the most gorgeous smile and beautiful teeth that complimented my presence. He was just what I needed to escape from my reality with A.H. What I didn't know was he had already spotted me when he was outside talking to his cousin, Donti. He had told him I was going to be his wife.

The party was jumping. Tye and I were dancing with each other, two-stepping and clowning while sipping on alcohol. Neither of us could stop smiling. People probably thought our faces were stuck.

Tye said, "Do you want to get up out of here to get some air?"

"Sure," I said.

So we walked downstairs onto the beach. Day was turning to night. We were just laughing and enjoying each other at the moment.

He then said in the most sincere tone, "If I could marry you tomorrow, I would."

I smiled and said, "That's just the liquor talking."

He said, "No, seriously."

In my head, I was like, *Yeah right*. We talked more and then headed back to the party. When it was over, he went to talk to my mom on the second floor. I was on the third floor watching something on *Investigation Discovery*, which was one of my favorite channels. I can't quite remember what was on but I remember the scene being intense. I was into it.

Suddenly, Mom came in and jumped on my back, scaring the mess out of me.

"Girl!"

Then she stepped back and covered her mouth.

I said, "What?"

She said, "Nidda!"

"What Mom, what is it?"

Mom could barely speak. She just stood there looking at me for a while.

"That man really loves you."

"Who, Tye?" I asked skeptically.

She replied, "Yes! He just asked me if he could marry you."

"Hold up. Mom, he's been drinking."

"No Nidda, this man loves you. He is serious."

I still didn't think he was serious. That night he and I laid in the bed together and we talked. I told him I was trying to leave a relationship. He told me if I needed help, I should let him know. He also told me he had a church engagement to go to the next day. A friend of his was putting on a play and they had asked him to mime at their church, to which he agreed. He asked me if I wanted to go with him. I said yes. We laid in each other's arms that night. He was very respectful and guess what, so was I.

Not long after making it back to Jacksonville, I realized that God does listen to people like me. You see, being raised as a Jehovah's Witness, I had to unlearn a lot of teachings that were half truths or not true at all. I knew enough to know that God existed but I didn't have complete faith in Him. I was totally confused. I couldn't understand why God, being so powerful and all knowing, could allow bad things to happen. I did not realize then that God does not want robots to love Him; he wants people to love Him. If he destroyed everyone who committed a sin when they did it, Christ going to the Cross would have been in vain. There would be no need for redemption. But because He is a just God and no sin is above the next, even I would have been destroyed a long time ago. I did not understand this then. All I knew was that I had been hurt one way or another by people who I knew, I trusted and loved God, and God let it happen.

Jehovah's Witnesses make you think you have to be

perfect when you come before God, and I was far from that. I would still talk to Him from time to time just in case He really did listen to sinners, and it seemed like He was.

My prayer got answered, because about two months later, the condo that I really wanted came through. Tye kept his promise and came down here to help me move. I insisted he stayed back, because I didn't want him and A.H. running into each other. Tye ended up giving me a taser gun as protection in case I needed it and sent his son, LaDedrick, who we call L.A. to help me move. L.A brought a family friend, Kenny, to also assist.

I called up U-haul and scheduled a pick up for when A.H. would be at work. We still worked at the same place but were on different schedules. L.A. brought Kenny, my nephew's father, to help me and the boys pack up. We got everything that I cared about except my laptop computer that my brother Charles bought me. He hid that somewhere during an argument, and I never recovered it. The U-haul was parked on the side of the house because it was an exit out to the next street. I got up out of the house so fast that I ended up driving the U-Haul into the side of the roof of the house. Man, if I had a quarter jar for the amount of times I dropped F-bombs, my boys would have their college tuition paid for that quickly.

That was the first and last time they have ever heard me be so explicit. I sped off and looked back only once to see the damage. I had mixed feelings about getting it fixed. I tell you, if it were not for his mom being as sweet and loving as she was, that roof would have remained damaged. But, because of my love for her, I called my cousin Jermaine and had him fix the roof. It hurt my heart that I wasn't going to see Tiana again. It felt as if I had just lost my daughter, which in a sense, I did. A.H. played on that emotion by stopping off work when he knew I was there one day. He came to "pick up something."

As he was leaving, he spoke out loud in my presence, "I need to go. I have my daughter Tiana in the car."

He knew how badly I wanted to see her, but I pretended to not care. To this day, I have never seen her again. Trina found out that we broke up. I don't think she knew exactly why at the time. All I know is that he found her on Facebook and friend requested her. She denied his request. I cracked up when she told me that. I filled her in on the details though. She and I don't talk much now, because we both live busy lives. It's unspoken but understood that we will always be there for each other.

After being settled into my condo for a month, I made the trip to Philadelphia. I had so much fun. Tye and I talked for hours as I was on my way. He wanted to make sure I was okay on the road and that I made it safely. He then told me he should come up there since it was only about six hours away. He was missing me, and I was missing him. Before Dot's birthday, Tye would still come to Jacksonville to visit because he had family here. With each visit, either he would have a girlfriend visiting with him or I would have boyfriends over.

It's funny because none of that mattered when our eyes connected. I didn't care about his girlfriends, and he didn't care about my boyfriends. When we wanted to flirt, it didn't matter who was around. In each other's eyes, we came first. I didn't understand this because he was supposed to be my play toy. Now, here we were dating again, and this time we weren't sneaking around. I wasn't sure how serious we could be, because there was one thing standing in the way: distance.

I lived in Florida, and he in North Carolina.

So I asked, "How are we going to do this?"

Jabari was only six years old, and Jamal would have fought me tooth and nail. We already couldn't hold a conversation without being at each other's throat. I told him there was no way I could leave Florida right now. He also told me that he couldn't leave either. Tye has three girls and L.A. He didn't want to leave them behind. He lived in Wilmington, and they lived in Greensboro. Although they weren't in the same city, he was still close to them and very active in their lives. It seemed all was lost and that this fairytale was over before it really began.

Then he reassured me, "We will figure something out."

I didn't see how that was possible being that neither of us were ready to budge.

I left Philadelphia a week later, as planned. I drove twelve hours by myself with Dasjuan and Jabari in the car. By the time

I arrived home, all I wanted to do was lay down. I literally had just walked in my condo door when my cell phone rang. I wasn't even good in the house yet. The call was from a 404 (Atlanta) area code.

I looked at my phone and said, "I don't feel like answering this," and threw the phone on the bed.

Something was telling me I should have answered that call, so I immediately grabbed my phone and listened to the voicemail.

"Hello Aishia, this is such and such from the set of *Reed Between the Lines*. We want you to have a walk-on role playing the role of the bus driver picking up kids…"

I listened to the rest of the message and tried my best to contact her back. I must have called back like a hundred times. I couldn't get in touch with her.

That was my chance, and I blew it! I typically live my life with no regrets, but at that time, this was my one regret. I called Tye and told him what had occurred. He comforted me and told me not to give up. He said there will be other chances.

So, five months after Tye and I dated long distance, he told me he had made the decision to move down here to Jacksonville to be with me. I was surprised because neither of us were willing to leave our families behind for one reason or another. I asked him if he was sure this was what he wanted to do. He said yes. He told me he was coming down on November

1, 2010.

Then he said, "I can't wait until I get there. I am going to be around you all day."

I tell ya, it was like the needle scratched the record. My ears must have gone up like a curious dog. I took the phone from my face and made the craziest side-eyed face that a human could make. *Did he just say he was going to be around me all day?* I thought. Oh heck no! I don't play that. I barely wanted to deal with myself all day, let alone some man. You see, in past relationships, I had my peaceful time. Either they were gone a lot or I was, but now you're talking about "all day!" We had a problem. I had no following comment. All I could do was think of those echoing words, "All day."

He came down as promised. Luckily for me, he quickly found a job in his long-standing career of barbering. That cut down that "all day" talk.

But then he started working late nights. He was at the barbershop from the time he got up until about eleven o'clock at night sometimes. He was doing what he had to do to build up his clientele. It was cool at first, and then it happened.

I started missing him. I started wanting him around more and more each day that I had developed a yearning to be in his presence. I finally understood what he meant when he said he wanted to be around me "all day." I began to experience feelings that I never knew existed within me. This man moved down here with an agenda.

He meant it when he said I was going to be his wife back in early June. One of the first things he wanted to do was to find a church home. Although I had lost my faith in churches after being raised as a Jehovah's Witness, I had gained enough faith in Tye to follow his lead. We visited three churches. We both agreed that the first church wasn't what we were looking for. We then visited the Potter's House church. He fell in love with it, because he said it reminded him of the church he attended back home in Wilmington, NC. I didn't care for it all. The atmosphere reminded me of being on a movie set with all of the cameras everywhere. Then to top it off, one of the preachers came up to preach, giving a sermon or a testimony.

He seemed to be fake crying while he was talking. I was so ready to walk up out of there at that moment. It seemed like we weren't going to find a church home, and quite frankly, I was okay with that. I went to work and while I was at lunch, I was clowning as usual with the twins, Tyrone and Jerome. They owned a sandwich shop inside of ERC. I knew Tyrone before they opened the sandwich shop because he used to be a collections manager there. He is always smiling. His personality is contagious and it seems as if nothing ever bothers him. He's been that way as long as I've known him. While I was getting my food in their sandwich shop, I mentioned how we were looking for a church home and told them some of the issues we were running into. Tyrone then proudly told me about his church, Mount Horeb Baptist Church. He said it was a smaller church, and the pastor was hands-on with all of his members. He said everyone is like family there which was appealing to me. He also told me they were non-traditional Baptists, so people could come as they are, and that they sang songs that were modern. That also caught my attention.

I went home and told Tye about it. We decided to visit the church and I loved it. I got the same feeling that I felt when I visited Shiloh except the choir was smaller. They were called a praise team and guess who was on it, Tyrone. I had no idea that he could sing! Then Pastor Simmons, the head pastor of the church, walked up to the pulpit to preach. He welcomed the new members. As he was giving the brief welcome speech, I got nervous. I thought he was going to tell us to stand up and/or introduce ourselves. *Here we go,* I thought. To my surprise, we did not have to stand up. He did not call us out. He just verbally welcomed us and continued preaching. I felt so relieved! *I can dig it!* I thought. Tye wasn't feeling it though. He wanted to attend Potter's House, and I wanted to attend Mount Horeb.

I asked Tye, "What will happen if we can't agree on a church home?"

He respectfully said to me he would make a decision as the man in our relationship, and I would have to follow him. The record scratched again! Did he just tell me that I had to follow him? *Please! I am an independent woman. Who are you to take my choice from me?* I thought. My next thought was, *That was kind of sexy though, dang!* I have never had anyone to speak so candidly with me, not like he did.

The following Saturday rolled around, and I asked, "So now what?"

He said we will visit Mount Horeb again. I don't know what happened in that second visit but he began to open up to the idea of that being our church home. After a few months, Tye told me he was ready to join the church. Pastor Simmons did the opening call for people who wanted to get saved and then a second call for those who wanted to join the church as he did every Sunday. Tye got up, I followed, and then we walked down the aisle. Surprisingly, I wanted to join after the first sermon but I needed to follow his lead.

I remember Dasjuan and Jabari being in the children's room when a member of the church told them to come out and join us at the front. We were then welcomed by everyone in the congregation. It was actually a great feeling.

June 24, 2011, Tye took me out to dinner for my birthday the day after I turned 33. We were enjoying each other's company when I noticed my friend and co-worker, Mario and his beautiful wife Raquel. They sat with us and we all had a beautiful dinner. Shortly following, Fhanta came in and sat with us. *What is going on,* I thought. Mario and Raquel could have been a coincidence, but Fhanta too? Yeah, something was definitely up. I then thought he was inviting them to join us for my birthday dinner. Tye then walked up to the DJ and grabbed the mic.

Fhanta started talking but I hushed her so I could hear what he had to say. He then called me to the dance floor; he got down on one knee and popped the big question. I never looked at myself as being a wife. As a matter of fact, I never wanted to get married. I saw my mom in a few failed marriages, and she was a good wife. I also saw people around me being happily in love, but after two years of marriage they are either divorced or contemplating it.

It just wasn't for me. I didn't want that responsibility. Besides, I was too independent and had too much play in me to be settled down to one person. But this was Tye. This man loved and respected me so much, and he didn't mind letting the world know.

He made me feel so secure. Anytime a beautiful woman was in our presence, he would make it known that he only had eyes for me. He would wrap his arms around me or grab my hand or do whatever he felt he had to to make me feel secure. I was never insecure, but he made sure he didn't give me a reason to be. He made sure he was an open book to me. He gave me his passwords to his phone. When he came home he would leave his phone around instead of babysitting it all day and night. He would even tell me to answer his phone when it rang and he wasn't near it. Whatever I needed, whether it was physical, emotional, mental or even spiritual, he did his best to provide it. I actually wanted to be perfect for him.

Even though I tried monogamy previously, he was the first guy that I actually succeeded with. I even stopped cursing cold turkey because I wanted him to keep me on a pedestal. It took a short while for me to answer. This was only because I was in shock with what was happening. Nevertheless, I said yes and meant it. We danced the night away afterwards. We danced so hard that I broke the heel of my shoe and I didn't care. A few days later, I started focusing on planning our wedding. We had planned to marry in June of the following year. I had everything picked out, from my bridesmaids dresses, to the colors that I wanted them to wear, to the song that I wanted to walk out on. I even had the type of flowers that I wanted in my bouquet.

We then met with our pastor for marriage counseling.

Following that meeting, Tye came to me and said, "I don't want to live in sin any longer. Let's get married sooner."

I said, "Okay, when?"

He wanted to get married as soon as possible. After we discussed some dates, we decided to get married within two weeks. We told our family and our pastor about our new plans. We then filed for our marriage license. That night we were at Checkers fast food restaurant. We had just left the drive thru and were about to turn onto Blanding Boulevard to head home.

We were talking about our future life and then I said, "I know we are going to have our arguments…"

Before I could finish my sentence, he looked at me and said, "Who's going to argue?"

Those few words changed my view on relationships. It was like the heavens opened and God himself thumped me on my head, because it finally hit me that arguing was a choice. He and I had both been in relationships where all we did was argue with our previous partners. We didn't have to bring that energy into this relationship. And there it was, Tye and I both made the choice to always speak to each other in a loving respectful tone, no matter what. Now, I will say that in the beginning there were times that I wanted to let him have it. Not that he deserved my verbal wrath, but because I was used to lashing out when things did not go a certain way. Instead of arguing, I would go in the shower and say everything that I wanted to say, how I wanted to say it, and then I would feel better. By the time I got out of the shower, I was able to go and talk to Tye calmly and with respect. I did this as often as I needed to until talking calmly became second nature.

My rule of thumb has always been: If it is not worth getting a divorce over, then the situation is not that serious.

This thought process kept the stupidity and ignorance out of our relationship.

Fhanta came through and rented a stretch limousine for

my bachelorette dinner. She planned the dinner and gathered some of my closest friends to celebrate with us. We rode in the limo from my friend's house to the Cheesecake Factory where we had the ultimate great time. My mom planned a surprise wedding for me. When I say surprise, I mean she went through my written down plans and followed everything to a T. She gathered all of my friends and had Tye's family come down from North Carolina. She did all of the decorating. She ordered the cake and got my Uncle Mann to DJ at our reception. I didn't have to lift a finger except to put my dress on, which my friends helped me with.

The night before, I stayed with my great friend, Arnitra. She and I are so close that we were more like sisters than friends. It was at her house that I received a call from my dad telling me how proud he was of me and that he wouldn't be able to make it to my wedding. His reasoning was due to his religious beliefs, he was not going into a church. At one time, Jehovah's Witnesses highly discouraged their members from going into churches. I guess because they didn't want other religious views to taint their beliefs. I was hurt but I didn't let it show. I told my mom why he wasn't coming, and she was not happy.

Mom wasn't about to let anyone upset her Nidda, especially right before her wedding. So, she got on the phone and had words with my dad. I told my mom that I wished my brother Charles could come and that my brothers would walk me down the aisle. I have a close relationship with mostly all of my brothers. If it were possible, I would have had my brother Rahual, my oldest brother from my dad, my brother Charles, and my brother Kahlil walk me down the aisle. But Charles still lived in California and Rahual lived in West Virginia.

    Nevertheless, the wedding was going to happen. Momma made sure the wedding started on time and that there were no mishaps. The day of my wedding, the limousine picked me and my bridesmaids up from my condo, including my sister Fhanta. They made sure everything went well and that I was not stressed. When I got to the church, they had me sit in the room separate from everyone until it was time to walk out. The music started for the ceremony. Then it was time for me to walk out. I stood by the door blindfolded. Kahlil grabbed my left arm and walked me to the center of the aisle. I knew it was him because I smelled Lebaron cologne. He always wore it just like my father. He let go, and then someone grabbed my right arm. This person had muscles. The blindfold was removed and I looked over to my right. Lo and behold, it was Charles! I wanted to cry. I was stiff.

    He whispered, "Are you gonna walk?"

    I held back my tears, but I was overwhelmed by his presence. My legs were weak, but I had to keep them strong as best as I could.

    When the Pastor asked who would give me away, he proudly said, "I do."

Every time I think about that moment, I get emotional. My family came through at the time I needed them the most. My dad let me down, but my brothers were right there to pick me back up as they had always been.

Then I saw my soon-to-be husband. He was standing there staring, in awe of me with those beautiful hazel eyes. My best friend Kutana stood as my Matron of Honor. My cousin Shonti and my sister Fhanta were my bridesmaids.

Our son (I could now use those words), L.A. stood as Tye's Best Man. Shonti's husband, Jermaine and his friend Alex, who owned the barbershop where he worked were the groomsmen. We said our vows and suddenly we became one. His children are now my children and vice versa. We had an understanding that we are not stepparents, we are parents. The beauty of it all is, I gained three daughters; guess what one of their names is: Tiana. When I left A.H. I knew I would never see his daughter Tiana again, and that broke my heart. Even though she is irreplaceable, God sent me another daughter with the same name bonded by a beautiful covenant and she will always be my daughter.

THE RIGHT RELATIONSHIP

Marriage was always sacred to me, although I never wanted to be placed into the marital category. Since I was there, I wanted to give my husband a special gift. I wanted it to have meaning and be unforgettable. I wanted to give him a part of me that no one else had access to. I remember my dad telling me when I was a teenager that sex was a gift to your spouse. He said it is to be secured until the time is right. Well, by the time we had this conversation, my innocence was already gone. So what could I give my husband that I hadn't already given away? I was no longer a virgin; I had given my time, energy, and my heart.

I still had two gifts left in the bag. They were fidelity and respect. I had cheated in every relationship, and my brain-to-mouth filter was turned off. I said whatever and did whatever I wanted to do without even thinking twice about it, not before and dang sure was not afterwards. I had roaming eyes and a flirtatious spirit. The crazy thing was, I tried to give these gifts to both of my son's fathers. They were undeserving and couldn't give me the same, so it was game on.

My husband was different. His presence demanded respect in the most loving way. The peace and security he gave me made me want to go above and beyond for him. My eyes were fixed only on him. To me, I married the finest man walking! Let's be real, I don't expect for anyone to agree with me on that last statement. If you did, we would have a problem. He is just perfect for me. I vowed that no matter what, I would never cheat nor disrespect my husband. I was finally giving my all and to someone who is worthy of it.

Within a few months of being married, we found out we were pregnant. My first two children came out of wedlock, so this pregnancy meant a lot to me. I wanted to feel I was doing things right. I was so hoping for a girl. Well, before the end of my first trimester, I started cramping really badly. I went to the hospital to find out what was going on.

I had miscarried the baby. I was devastated. I tried not to show it emotionally. However, my body wouldn't allow me to hide what I was truly feeling inside. I was sick! Tye apparently felt the same way because he became nauseous. He could barely stand as his body leaned up against the hospital walls. This miscarriage drew Tye and I closer together as he became even more attentive to my needs, and I to his.

Shortly after, I received a call from my friend Kenny telling me he was coming to Jacksonville in a few days and wanted to link up. He was anxious for me to meet his fiance. She wanted to go shopping here, which was the reason for their visit. She and I had small talk on the phone a few times and she seemed to have a good spirit. I was excited to meet her. I had a crush on Kenny in middle school. I believe the feeling was mutual but nothing ever came of it. He had the most beautiful long eyelashes and thick eyebrows. I used to call him Snuffleupagus, like the character from Sesame Street.

He and I continued our friendship over the years although we did lose contact for a long while. I think we reunited on Facebook, and that's when I found out he moved back to Georgia. He called me back within a few days of that conversation and told me he wasn't going to make it, because he had cancer. He had it before and it recurred. I immediately talked to my husband about going to visit him. Tye was so supportive although he had never met or talked to him. As a matter of fact, I believe the first time he heard Kenny's name was when I asked if we could take that trip.

We drove to Georgia to visit him. He was in the military hospital and was in good spirits when we got there. We talked about his fiance and how they met; we caught up on old times and reminisced on our Stillwell days. He even told me that he found peace and that he was fine with whichever way this sickness turned out, because he was a Christian now. It was such a pleasant visit, but we had to get back to Jacksonville. It was getting late. I called him again to check on him only to find out that things had gotten progressively worse.

The next time I called him, I was met by his fiance's voice telling me his body had succumbed to the disease. My friend was gone. I immediately called my best friend, Kutana as she too went to school with Kenny. We drove to Georgia for our final goodbyes. I was extremely tired driving up there. The closer we got to Columbus, the faster I'd drive but not exceeding eighty five miles per hour. I got pulled over while en route. I told the police we were headed to a funeral, and he gave me a pass. I ended up pulling over to get a five hour energy shot to help me get through. I wasn't going to play with the Georgia police; with the help of the energy shot, I obeyed the speed limit. Usually they would work, but for some reason I ended up taking like three of them between coming and going. When we got back home, I slept like a baby!

Tye and I later discussed whether we wanted to try for another baby. At first, I wanted to. Then, I realized that our children were almost grown. We were almost retired parents. We both agreed that we didn't want any more children. By the end of that week, I was taking another pregnancy test and guess what?

It was positive. I literally looked up to the sky and thought, *God, you're funny*! Then I realized why the energy shots did not work.

Once again, we were excited because what was done was done. I prayed for a girl since I already had two boys biologically. I wanted a girl, because I knew she would be beautiful and have similar features like my other two handsome sons. I hoped she would have long hair like me so that I could do different hairstyles with it. I also wanted someone to go get manicures, pedicures, and do "girly" things with. Two boys and a girl is something that I've wanted since I was a teenager. I always said I would have the two boys first then the girl last. That way, the boys could protect the girl.

When I prayed for my girl, my husband went behind me and prayed for a boy. Men can be so sneaky. He already has three girls. Even though he has an older son, he wanted a son that bore his name. At four months the verdict was in. We both were filled with excitement. We joked about being God's favorite. I sat on the table while the sonographer put the cold jelly on my belly. We could hear the baby's heartbeat. We looked at each other and smiled. We knew that no matter the sex, the most important thing was that the baby was healthy. We were watching the body parts on the 2D monitor. It's time for his photoshoot.

"Bottoms up!" She took a snapshot.

We looked at the face. Snap! His thumb was in his mouth. Snap!

"Look at those thighs! They are shaped just like his dad's, so defined," I said.

Snap! Now for the moment of truth. I began to smile. It was the smile of defeat.

"What is that dangling in between those legs?"

It was all good though because he was my lil man regardless.

Reflecting back on my pregnancy with TJ, it was a breeze, but he was a result of baby fever. I was seeing everyone with babies and it made me want one with my husband. This was before I changed my mind. I made sure that baby fever would never be a thought again. I told my doctor I wanted a c-section followed by getting my tubes tied.

I told him I didn't want him taking any breaks after the surgery, "Get these babies tied!" I said.

Our son was scheduled to be born on May 1st. Tye's grandparents' wedding anniversary was on May 2nd so he asked me if I could push the delivery date back by one day. Tye's grandparents raised him. Because it was important to him, I honored his request. We had to be at the hospital at six thirty that morning so it wasn't a big deal to hold him in for a few more hours. The morning of, Doctor Garcia greeted me. He delivered my younger siblings from my mother and a few of her grandchildren, including Dasjuan, so I had complete trust in him. He sat me on the silver table and gave me a shot in my spine. After a few moments, I didn't feel anything. Doctor Garcia instructed me to push. I gave it all I had! My mom, Dot, my husband, and my children were my support system in the delivery room that day. Our son was named after his father, Tyrone Lendell McQuillan. We now had a Junior. We were going to call him TJ for short. TJ arrived on the scene at 8:23 that morning. He came into the world demanding attention and to this day is still demanding it. TJ was handsome like his brothers with perfect features. People are often confused about his ethnicity because of his complexion and flawless features. Some think he is Hawaiian, others think he is Puerto Rican, Indian, or even Samoan. He is simply black. His hair is long and wavy, and it continues to grow like wildfire. Before long, people were referring to him as Samson (from the Bible), because it was so long. It is past his butt! He participates in sports too such as soccer, football, and track & field, so we often go out and get massages together. Oh and I made the mistake of taking him with us when my husband and I got pedicures. He fell in love! At the end of the day, Tye and I both got what we wanted. It just took time and patience for me to receive my end of the deal.

Even though the delivery process was a breeze, the healing wasn't. I went through two other deliveries, but I have never had to endure the excruciating pain that I did with this one.

I went through over two months of intense suffering. I am one who has a high tolerance for pain, but I wouldn't wish this kind of pain on my worst enemy. Mom came by everyday for the first two weeks to help out with the baby while Tye went back to work. I thank God for mothers, because there is nothing like a mother's touch in your time of need. When I was finally able to bathe, Mom sat me down in a warm tub to help alleviate cramps and wash my back. It didn't bother her that I was older and had women parts that she didn't want to see. The only thing she cared about was taking care of her Nidda.

My husband felt so helpless. He and the boys catered to any and everything that I asked. All the while, I soldiered up and handled the task set before me with TJ. Everyone took care of me while I took care of TJ.

As I reflect on things introspectively, I've come to realize the significance in the births. You see, after Tye and I found a church home, I vowed to not play with God. I said if I was going to do it, I would go all in. Tye and I went before the altar shortly after joining the church, and we accepted Jesus Christ as our Lord and Savior. As a symbol of our dedication, we got baptized. During this time, I was still listening to rap and R&B. I would get around my girls and we would have a few sips of alcohol. I might take a few shots, as I was the shot queen. Then, I would go to church on Sunday and praise it up. I would listen intensely and be all into the word. I would even be excited to receive it but when people were praising and shouting I would say in my head, *It doesn't take all of that*. I didn't understand it because growing up as a Jehovah's Witness, we didn't do any of that. We would mostly sing in a monotone voice, and we definitely didn't do any shouting.

Every now and then, when service was over, Tye would turn to gospel instead of DMX or one of our other favorite rap artists. One day after leaving church service, Tye had it on a Gospel station. I was staring out of the window when I heard a familiar song that I heard a thousand times, but this time it was different. The song was called, *I Almost Let Go* by Kurt Carr. The words touched me deeply in a way they never had before. I had a quick, lightning flashback of my childhood and everything changed. I realized who kept me all of those years. When I thought I had no one, God was there the whole time. That's how I was able to keep going. That's why I never had suicidal thoughts. That's why I'm not reliant on any suppressants or depressants, and the list goes on!

I no longer desired to listen to rap music or anything that wasn't uplifting. I no longer wanted to take shots of alcohol. I still drank from time to time, but I was a social drinker. I even kept that to a minimum. I decided that I was not going to pursue my acting career anymore. I still had a passion for it, but if the project wasn't uplifting or required me to compromise my Christianity, I wasn't doing it. Unfortunately, that was most of the gigs that I was booking. I did decide that I would continue to write movie scripts, and if an acting gig came along that I was comfortable doing, I would take it. But that never happened.

I was changing for the better, and it felt great. Before I knew it, I was slow to anger. Ever since Jamal and I split, he had been a thorn in my side. We couldn't hold a conversation without arguing. It got to a point where I started praying for him. Before then, I used to ask God to remove the thorns from my life. But even my prayers began to change. I asked God not to remove the thorns but to ease the thorns in my side for as long as I had to endure them.

During my transformation, God was calling Tye to ministry. Tye talked to our pastor about what's been placed on his heart. To his surprise, Pastor Simmons told him that he and our reverend had already known about it before Tye came to him. It's amazing that not only did God speak to Tye about this but He confirmed it with our Pastor and our Reverend at different times before Tye even mentioned it. Tye was eventually given materials to study for the ministerial class. I was super excited for him but nervous at the same time, because this would mean my status would change. I would be classified as First Lady, and by no means was I the typical First Lady. I made a lot of changes but still had a ways to go. The street mentality wasn't too far from me. I was still working on that. *Besides, will I have to sit in the first row and wear big hats that obstruct the view of others?* I thought.

I knew the answer to that before I finished asking, but my mind was just crazy like that to even let me finish the thought. I remember when he finished the class, Tye had to stand in front of a panel of Pastors and answer questions regarding his knowledge of the Word and his love for Jesus. He then got his license to be a minister. He later followed the same steps to become an ordained minister, but this time he was in front of the church. I carried TJ in my arms as I stood side by side with my husband as he went through the acknowledgement of being ordained. I was the proudest wife ever! This was the moment I made a decision to stop drinking. Let me be clear, drinking isn't a sin; drunkenness is. However, the Bible elucidates this in 1 Timothy 3; it says that Bishops (some bible versions say Overseers, while others say Pastors; either way, my husband falls into this category) are not allowed to partake in any wine, whereas Deacons are not to partake in much wine. Since my husband had to give it up, I made the decision to stand alongside him and give it up as well. Not everyone was accepting of that but I didn't care.

My life was changing. Everyone could see it. Even my mom. When my mom noticed the change in me, she decided to change some of the ways she was living too. She went back to being a Jehovah's Witness. I tried to tell her all of the things I found out about that religion, like how they are called a pedophile's paradise because of all of the sexual abuse cases that they are covering up. I wanted her to see that I'm not an apostate like the Witnesses want them to believe. I follow the true living God, Jehovah and I am not a liar. I am living proof, but the more I spoke and told her to research for herself, the more she turned a deaf ear. She told me that she would never leave Jehovah's side again. Although I didn't agree I respected her decision and left it alone. I wished she understood that leaving the religion wasn't leaving God's side. God is not attached to any religion. He is attached to relationships. I was hurt deeply to know that she supports the same religion that's still fighting in court today becauses of allegations from all around the world with different victims. To me, if you don't condone that behavior but you're still supporting the organization, you're just as guilty as the perpetrators. Turning a blind eye doesn't make situations go away. It just makes you foolish to the facts. That's just like when the crowd was yelling "Crucify him!" speaking about Jesus. They didn't personally nail him to the cross; but they were just as guilty, because they supported the crucifixion. Nevertheless, our difference in religion only drew a hairline fracture in our relationship. Before, we reached a point where we could talk about anything. Now, we have limits before the conversation goes sideways.

In this Christian walk, I have grown so much in time. I have even gotten to the point where I forgave every last perpetrator. This was the hardest thing for me to do. I didn't want to, but then I thought about Jesus. I thought about how we have done worse things to Him, and He still forgives us.

After that revelation, I knew what I had to do.

I sucked it up and with each name I said those words, "I forgive you."

With all of that being said, I now understand the significance of the intensity and longevity of pain that I endured while I was healing. You see, I was not just giving life to TJ; I was giving life to myself, a renewed life. But that was the easy part because I had help. My husband has always been my comforter. The hard part was the part that no one could help me with. The healing. I wasn't just healing in the body; I was going through a complete recovery. I was healing physically, emotionally, mentally, and spiritually! I was releasing all of the hurt and pain from my past.

I'm starting to understand that my worst pains in life end up being a blessing in disguise one way or another.

Aishia McQuillan

HIS HANDS

Growth of any type comes at a cost. I realized that in order for me to grow into the person that I was trying to be, I had to cut some people off. I backed away from a lot of people, including my best friend, Kutana. I never had a fallout with anyone. I just stopped initiating contact. If anyone needed me, I made myself available to them but I needed to focus on me. Kutana must have been working on herself as well; as soon as we did get back in contact with each other, she had become Christian, too.

Coming out of my seclusion, I noticed that the people who I had associated myself with would no longer invite me to certain outings.

When I found out about them, the excuse would be, "Well, I knew you were busy."

Shockingly, these same people also claimed Christianity.

The difference was our walk looked different.

In biblical times, the title of "Christian" was offensive to those who followed Christ. Christians didn't call themselves that, other people did. So when you have Christians who proclaim the name but the walk is the same as the world's, the authenticity of their Christianity must be in question. Knowing this, I was okay with being left out. Obviously something was going down that I didn't need to be a part of anyway. This was why I didn't mind being different or outcasted. Not only that, but I was so used to people close to me coming in and out of my life. That makes it easier to feel unbothered.

At the same token, if people couldn't respect my spiritual change, I didn't want to be around them anyway.

My family was different though. Most of my paternal family were still Jehovah's Witnesses, my mom was one as well, so it was a constant battle when it came to religious truths.

My paternal grandmother would always ask me in her sweetest voice, "Nik, when are you gonna come back to the truth? I really wish you'd come back to Jehovah."

My grandmother is my world! I love her dearly, and I don't ever want to disappoint or upset her.

So, I politely responded, "Mommom, I have the truth because I have Jesus."

I could hear the disappointment in her voice, because it wasn't the response she was looking for. As a matter of fact, those conversations were the only times in life I had ever let her down. It didn't feel good, but I knew I must stand up for what is right, no matter the cost.

Then there were my parents. Well, we let each other down our whole lives, though unintentional. My dad and I went at it all the time, but he and I were still two peas in a pod. If he dished it out, I took it. If I dished it out, he took it. I never crossed the line with my dad, but I did skate in the grey area way too often when we got into our religious conversations. It was aggravating because my dad always thought he was right even when I knew I proved him wrong. He wouldn't admit it though. He would continue on, and we had to agree to disagree more than likely. That was a technique I learned over time while speaking with people who don't believe the same things as you do; agree to disagree. Because when it comes to God's Word, it's not you who they are disputing, especially when you are showing them something straight from the Bible itself.

As far as Mom was concerned, I'll never forget when I hurt her in the worst way, but I had to stand up for what was right. I'm not one to do something just to please others so if someone was hurt by something I did or said it was because I stood firm in my belief. This time, my husband and I traveled to Jamaica because Arnitra was getting married. We had my mom watch TJ for the week that we were to be gone. Dreadfully, I had to tell my mom that if something happened to me and Tye while we were gone and we did not make it back, TJ was to live with his godparents. Mom didn't understand why, and it hurt her so much. She cried, and because she loves TJ dearly, I cried too. Mom does not cry, so to hear her on the phone sniffling, I knew I had hurt her deeply. I wish I could have taken back those words. Sometimes I wish I was better at sugar coating things so that I could soften the blow. That's just not my expertise. Normally, I am unphased after a few seconds of an incident, but this one took me a few days to get over.

My mom is my everything, my queen! I quickly tried to get her to see that it wasn't the difference in religion but more so their doctrine that devalued Jesus' deity that could cause my son to lose his salvation. She wasn't trying to hear it. As a matter of fact, she politely ended the conversation with me. I wanted to call her back, but I just gave her space.

Here's the thing, I knew I was following the right path, because of the spiritual encounters that I had with God. This was not to say that everyone who followed God would have the same spiritual gifts as me. God does not want our gifts to be uniform. He has given some people the gift to teach; some people He has blessed with a generous heart but for me; He has given me the gift of prophecy. This is not like a fortune teller; however, I would dream things and they would come true.

The first dream I remember was about my best friend Kutana. She and I had lost contact with each other sometime after Jabari was born. We hadn't talked for over five years, maybe longer. I would dream of her trying to get in contact with me. These dreams became more frequent as the months progressed. Before you know it, I received a call from Fhanta saying that I had a letter at my mom's house from Kutana. I thought she was lying. I immediately went over there to get the letter. It had Kutana's number on it so I called her. We caught up on old times. My mom's address was publicly listed at the time which is how she found us. After talking with Kutana, I realized that the closer it was to her contacting me, the more frequent the dreams had become. When I told my mom about this, she told me we had psychics in our family.

I said to myself, *I am not a psychic; they are not of God*. I had no religion at that time, but I knew that much.

There was also another time before my husband came into my life that I dreamt that I was outside around a group of people. The people were separated into two circles. The top circle contained a small group of people. I was in that group along with a man who felt like he belonged to me. He was blurry though. The only people that I recognized were my biological children, but at some point they were a blur. There were other children and people around us that I didn't know. Then there was a circle below us, but it had a much larger number of people. It was crazy, because there were familiar faces in the bigger circle. However, I felt safe and comforted where I was. I had no idea what that meant at the time. That dream made absolutely no sense so I chalked it up as normal.

It took years for me to understand it. One Sunday, I was chilling with my husband after church service. My bonus children were visiting for the summer from North Carolina when it finally hit me. God had reminded me of the dream I'd had a few years earlier. He was showing me that he was bringing me a husband. My husband was coming with children. He also showed me that we will be separated from the world by our Christianity. He showed me that there would be far less people in our circle of salvation. I immediately told my husband about that dream, but I think it went in one ear and out the other.

I would continue to tell my husband out about my dreams and how they would come true. He never believed me. Sometimes the abnormal becomes ostracized because of its position, but abnormal doesn't mean impossible. People tend to forget that. My husband was one of those people. He thought I was making this up. There was nothing I could do to convince him that I was telling the truth, because it wasn't happening to him or anyone he knew. That was a bit disappointing to me, but it was only a matter of time before he'd see for himself. It was inevitable, because we were married.

In 2013 we were in the process of buying our house. Everything was going wrong! I had a shared account with Tot to help her out for personal reasons. It just so happened that her account got messed up at the wrong time. We went through hell and high waters to get it corrected. There were other things going on that I don't quite remember. I do remember feeling discouraged, because it seemed as if we weren't going to get approved for the home loan.

One night, I dreamt we were going to get our home but six things had to happen first. I can't remember what they were now. I woke up the next morning, thinking nothing special about the dream. I felt the urge to detail this dream to him, mentioning all six events. Before we knew it, three of those things had happened in real life!

I effusively said to my husband, "Bae, do you remember my dream?"

He couldn't believe it! Neither could I. We watched the events I'd dreamed of continue to unfold before us, and the house was ours. From that day forward, he was a believer. I also made it a point to tell him every dream that I remember just so he could understand that it wasn't a one-time occurrence. I was stupid excited about what happened, so I called my mom up.

She skeptically said, "Um, Nik, are you serious?"

I said, "Yes!"

"Who do you think you are, Moses or someone? Why would he single you out?"

She completely stole my joy! I couldn't believe what I was hearing, especially from my mom. She had been my main supporter my whole adult life! She was my go-to for everything. I still tried to convince her though. I needed her to see what I was seeing.

Then she said, "God doesn't speak to people today."

It was at that point I realized that even though people call themselves Christians, not everyone was on the same spiritual level.

If God does not talk to people today, what is the purpose of prayer? When did God stop talking to people? I know there was a period of four hundred years of silence between the old testament and new testament but God started communicating with us again and has never stopped. These were my thoughts as I listened to her tear me down as if I was crazy.

I called my husband following our conversation. He provided as much comfort as he could in that moment. He told me that I couldn't share my spiritual experiences with everyone. He told me that some people try to limit God's powers. They say He is all powerful and can do all things but don't actually believe in their heart. He told me I cannot make her see what she doesn't want to see.

Here's where I went wrong: I was obsessed with wanting to be heard. As a believer, that shouldn't have been my priority. When I told her and she didn't believe, that should have been the end of it. James 1:19 tells us to be quick to listen, slow to speak, and slow to get angry. I read somewhere that when we doubt God, that speeds up our mouth and slows down our mind. Since that day, this was something that I had to meditate on and put into practice to become a better being.

Mom's disbelief didn't stop my relationship with God. He continued to show me things. Some things I had to react to, like being a messenger for others, while others things were for my own knowledge. For instance, some time ago, I ended up being a victim of a scam and lost a lot of money believing in a system that didn't work. During this time, I dreamt I was in a pool, and the water was above my nose. I could still breathe. I realized later God was telling me that I was in deep, but I wasn't going to drown. That is exactly what happened.

But then there was a time when Nadia, a friend and member of my church, was diagnosed with cancer. She was calm, she had faith and she was still concerned for others while she was in the hospital suffering. Her actions were the ultimate definition of what true faith looked like. Well, I dreamt of her one night. I dreamt that not only was she going to beat cancer, but she was going to leave the hospital early.

I called her up the next day and told her about my dream. I then told her that it was just a dream, because treatment had to run its course. After we hung up the phone, my heart was pricked by the Holy Spirit. He made me realize what I had said to her. I basically said that cancer was above God. I quickly repented and called her back to apologize. I told her that I was wrong for saying that because no illness is above God. Guess what? Nadia did get out of the hospital early and has been cancer-free ever since.

It's times like these when I think about what my mom asked me, "Do you think you're Moses or somebody?"

Initially, I was offended and hurt when she first said that, but the more I grew into my faith, the more I saw that as a compliment. Prior to Moses' encounter with the Lord, he was a murderer and a doubter. He had a speech impediment, and felt unworthy of fulfilling the task that God wanted him to do. It wasn't until he got to know God that he became the Moses that led the Jews out of slavery.

I may not be Moses, but I am a standard being like Moses. I've done my dirt, and I feel just as unworthy. However, when God is present in your life, you can go on to do great things just like Moses. However, having these gifts comes with a responsibility. I admit that I am not in God's word like I should be or like I want to be. I'm sure that this is the reason that I can't always differentiate a regular dream from a prophetic one until something that I dream comes true. The last prophetic message I received in my sleep was about our pastor's children. I remember calling his wife, Tanisha and telling her about it. She was surprised, because I had both of her daughters' personalities dead on in my dream. We cracked up about it. But, we got so consumed in our conversation that I forgot to give her the full message about her son, EJ. I did tell her a little bit, and I believe it had something to do with his college career choice. At the time I dreamt that he was in his last year in high school, and I don't think he had decided what school he was going to yet. If he had, I did not know but in my dream, it was a college close to home. I remember him looking happy and comfortable in my dreams. Tanisha and I were enjoying our conversation so much that by the time we ended the call I realized I had forgotten to tell her the second part of the message which was that he was going to be okay. I thought, *I'll call her later and tell her*. I never did. I thought about it several times afterwards and continued to push it off. I convinced myself that it didn't matter anyway. Well, that was the last time I had a prophetic dream. A year and some change later, a group of us were discussing EJ after service had ended. Pastor Simmons showed us a video of EJ in a marching band. EJ is only a freshman in college but he had earned a spot on the front line in the band within a couple of weeks. We stood around verbally celebrating his success when suddenly, I was convicted of my failed task. I talked to Tye about it on the drive home. He suggested that I still call Tanisha to let her know. I did just that when I got home and apologized to her for not giving her the message sooner. I explained how I kept putting it off thinking that it was minute. She shared with me how she was worried for him initially because he thought about going to a different school that was farther away and that they weren't comfortable with, but she stayed in prayer and over time she felt relieved. God had been told me to deliver that message to her and maybe I could have saved her from the worry but I didn't listen and I failed at the mission. Thankfully, she is a praying woman. This was a reminder for me that God's Will doesn't change because of unwilling participants.

I hadn't had another prophetic dream since. You see, this has happened before when I was supposed to give someone a message. I put it off, because I deemed it as unnecessary. I prayed about it and told God that if he didn't shut me out that I would make sure I carried out the duties set before me. It wasn't for my glory. I understood that this was a spiritual gift that God had given me freely. Out of all of the people in the world, he chose me. I didn't want to lose that.

Although it's been a while since I had a vision, I still do get premonitions that guide and direct me. I've come to realize that TJ does too. There were times that he would tell me about dreams that would come true, but they would be little things. The one that sticks out to me wasn't a dream but a feeling. I had custody of my nephew at this time. TJ and my nephew Caleb were outside playing by the corner of the house. We live in a pretty decent neighborhood where nothing ever happens. One day TJ got a strong feeling that he couldn't shake. He told Caleb that they needed to get back home, because he had a feeling someone was going to get shot. My nephew didn't want to leave initially, but TJ told him again so they ran home and told me about it.

That was a crazy feeling, I thought.

Within minutes, I received an alert on my phone from the Nextdoor Neighborhood app that a female was shot at the corner of my house in a domestic dispute. I gasped! God had warned my son what was going to happen. Had he not listened, they could have been caught in a crossfire, traumatized, or who knows! I was talking to some people about this incident in a group that I am in on Facebook. Of course, most everyone was skeptical of my story.

Of course I got the, "Why would God save your son when others are dying or suffering?"

I also got, "It could have been intuition," and other ignorant comments that discredited God. But God has proven his existence to me on multiple occasions.

He has proven this to others as well. The problem is when you don't believe, you miss the answers that you're seeking. I don't know why God chose my son out of all of the many others, but I do know I am indebted. I also know it couldn't be intuition, because I try my best to keep my son innocent. Everything he sees and hears is kid-friendly. Our neighborhood is peaceful. I hang out with like-minded people, so the times when he is left with someone, they practice the same principles as we do at home. I can't protect him from everything, but the positive that he is exposed to far exceeds the negative. It shows in everything he does. So for him to say that someone is going to get shot, and it happens within minutes, was not instinctive. It was God!

I still share these experiences with Mom, because she is my best friend. At times, the psychics in our family would still come up. Other times she'll make comments as if I am unworthy to be chosen by God. As of late, she just listens and keeps her thoughts to herself. But let's look at some of the people God chose to do His Will: Moses was a murderer; Thomas was a doubter; Matthew was a tax collector; Judas betrayed Jesus; Paul persecuted Christians. Yet God found all of them worthy. My question is, when did He stop being God? He didn't. Apparently, there is something He sees in me that He can use the way He used them. I've gladly accepted the responsibility.

This is why comments like those no longer bother me. I've come to understand that spiritual battles are necessary in order for your faith to grow. Most victories aren't seen overnight, if at all. Christians often feel like they have failed if they don't see instant results. This is where I often found myself when I talked to my Jehovah Witness family about my Christian walk or even about my spiritual encounters with God. No matter what the outcome may be, I have to remember to embrace God's plans for me and understand that what He has for me is not for anyone else. I am safely placed in God's hands, and He has proven this to me on more than one occasion. There is nothing that believers, half-believers, or non-believers can tell me otherwise. I also have to remember that we plant seeds, but God does the watering and makes them grow. Just because my family does not see now, doesn't mean they never will. Cedric brought me to his church twelve years ago. To this day, he has no idea that he was the plantsman. God used my husband to water and grow me. It's not always meant for us to know the outcome, just be obedient and do the work that God has assigned for us to do.

A TEST OF FAITH

I faced many battles with my mom when I told her that God speaks to me in my dreams. Most of them are because she doesn't believe that God talks to people today. Here's the thing, God may not stand before us like he did back in Moses' day in His full Glory to bless us with his thunderous voice.

Although personally, I do recall a time when I was in a deep sleep and heard a thunderous voice that said, "Get up!"

When I woke up, the house was empty. I wasn't a Christian at that time so I was not sure if that was God's voice. After reading the account in 1st Samuel chapter 3 when God called Samuel three times in his dreams and he wasn't sure if that was His voice, Eli told him to say, "Lord, is that you." I said to myself that if this ever happened to me again, I would be sure to ask the same question, "Lord, is that you?" Anyway, we can't be too hard on Mom because many people feel the way she does. What people fail to understand is that God speaks to us through our thoughts, dreams, and feelings. His voice resonates with us and gives us peace in any situation, no matter how stressful it may become. The barrier that most face is that we don't listen. God isn't going to talk over you; you must place yourself in a position where you allow God to lead and you follow. God also knows each and every one of us. He created us so of course He does. So, for me, He chooses to communicate mostly by way of dreams. When I sit still for long enough, He will send me a strong irrefutable feeling.

This particular incident, I was still working at ERC. Tammy Hatfield was the HR Manager. I asked if she remembered me from Bombardier capital; she did. She also remembered the incident and told me that she hated to have to fire me over that. By this time, I had been promoted to recruiter and had been in this position for about three years. I didn't work under Tammy though. I started out under Jamie Jutte, who was the best Recruiting Manager ever. He got promoted then Liza took over. I loved Liza as a person, but I heard rumors that appeared to have some validity that she didn't like men. She seemed to be ruthless with them.

I never knew what each individual story was, but I'll never

forget when I heard her tell a male employee "Do you think we need you? We have computers that can do your job. You're replaceable."

I was like, *Dang! remind me not to get on her bad side.* I was glad I am female, and it wasn't my business so I stayed out of it. But then Mario, the one who was at my engagement dinner, got demoted. He was a great recruiter. He and I made an awesome team. For the life of me, I couldn't understand why. Talk about added pressure! Liza and Jessica called me into the office. Jessica was my supervisor. They wanted to let me know that I now had to recruit from both local offices. My workload substantially increased. However, I was only given a hundred dollar pay increase. I lived on the west side of town and had to travel to both offices on opposite sides of town. Doing this with two children and no solid babysitter everyday was hectic, but God worked it out daily. It got to a point where I contemplated if my salary was even worth it.

I thought about it long and hard until one morning I was listening to the *Steve Harvey Morning Show* on the radio. He was talking about staying put. He said sometimes God wants you to stay put in a situation, because there is work for you to do in that situation or lessons for you to learn. The words "stay put" echoed in that segment. I remember being on Baymeadows Road at the light when suddenly, it felt like Steve's hologram image came into my car and said, "Stay put." I knew then that God was sending me a message. Things started to take a turn for the worse. Liza couldn't read the Standard Operating Procedure so she started changing them. She would tell us to do things the normal way, meaning how we always did things.

When we did that, she'd tell us, "When I say 'normal,' that's not what I mean."

Even my supervisor was confused. Things got chaotic. I went from feeling like the best recruiter to the worst. I felt incompetent, but it wasn't me. Three weeks after Mario's demotion, my supervisor called me in the office with my boss on the phone and asked me to think about stepping down. I asked if this was a situation where I was being forced to or was this, *Aishia, you're stressed, think about stepping down and let us know?*

They told me I was being forced. There was no way I was going back to being a collector. I worked my butt off for that company for four years. I was so upset. Against my norm, I was compelled to send an email to the top executives to express my dissatisfaction at what had happened. I explained how I didn't want to come to them sooner in fear of committing career suicide. I received a message back from one of the female executives, Kim, who asked me to come in to see her. I was leaving for Philadelphia when she wanted me to come, but I assured her that I would be there as soon as I returned.

When I finally met with her, I found out that these ladies weren't supposed to demote neither me nor Mario. Based on their versions of complaints, they were supposed to find us a different position within the company. Mario and I had already made a positive name for ourselves, but they only had one version of the story to go off of. I was baffled and felt bad for Mario; because although he was a good collector, he was an awesome recruiter. He didn't deserve to be on the collector's floor. After speaking with Kim she found a position for me at the Bayberry office on the Southside in their Payment Processing center. I did lose a dollar in pay, but that beat losing two dollars like they tried to offer me in the demotion process. With everything seeming to go wrong, I still did not understand why I needed to "stay put".

I enjoyed working in the department. I was constantly on the computer analyzing data and working with numbers. Only God could put me in a position like this, because I hate math! Yet, I was put into a position for another four years where I was dealing with it daily.

Now at this point in my life, Tye and I had just started our Christian journey. I was also probably about two years working in my new position. One day I suddenly had this strong urge to stop working and start writing. I grabbed the legal pad that sat next to me on my desk and a pen, and the words started flowing. Before you know it, I had half of the script written and I already had the title. It was called *The Killer in the Mirror*. I finished it within two weeks. The screenplay is about a middle class family who had a teenage son who always found himself in troubled situations. He never started trouble. But due to his association, he was always in the midst of chaos. One day, trouble found its way to the house and tested the Christian faith of the whole family. I guess it was in God's plan for me to "stay put" and write the script at this job. This was probably the best place for me to concentrate and get it done.

I was proud of that script. There were moments where I had writer's block and had to pull in my husband's help. Those were for the filler scenes. We always made a great team. We got to the point where we were ready to go into production. We found the cast and the crew, but the crew wasn't so reliable. Then I ended up pregnant with TJ and had to put the whole thing on hold.

When TJ was born, Jabari was ten and in fifth grade. Dasjuan, who we also refer to as Scooby, was fourteen years old and a Sophomore in high school. When Scooby was younger, he had a complex about himself, because he was of a darker complexion than me and Jabari. Not only that, most of his family members were lighter. He got his complexion from his father, but his father was in and out of his life. That was something else we dealt with. As a result of these issues, Dasjuan went through episodes of cutting. Cutting is when a person inflicts physical pain by cutting themselves to temporarily alleviate mental or emotional pain. As handsome as he was, he didn't understand the beauty in being dark even though his complexion is smooth and beautiful.

I called my brother Charles, who still lived in California, to talk to him, as well as my dad who lived in Philadelphia. Both are of darker complexions and both give great advice. I also wanted him to speak man to man with family members who he respects. These talks provided him comfort but not enough confidence.

It wasn't until we stumbled upon a Walmart in a predominantly white neighborhood where I was walking through the clothes section to dodge a crowd and a white lady walked up to us and said to Scooby, "You are one handsome fella!"

His whole world changed. His eyes lit up.

He said, "Ma, did you hear that, she said I was handsome."

I had been telling him that his whole life; other people had been telling him that as well, but it wasn't enough. It took this woman of another race to tell him that he was handsome, and it changed his life. His walk changed in that moment, and little did I know, it changed him forever. From then on, homeboy thought he was the finest thing on earth. I lived in the joy of that moment. I found that lady in the store, thanked her, and shared his lack of confidence. She told me she was a teacher, and she understood kids. She said he was just so handsome that she was compelled to tell him.

Fast forward. Although Scooby continued to walk in confidence, he still respected women. He was never the player type and loved hard whether it was with someone he was dating or just a homie. If he loved you, he was loyal. But when he cuts you off, you're done. He is that guy who gives advice to others or lends the helping hand, even when he doesn't have it all together himself.

But he kept his friends to a minimum. His solid set of friends started out with Laman, who he had been cool with since childhood. Laman lived in the same neighborhood as my sister Tot. Actually, before Laman's mom passed, she and Tot were really good friends. So it's no surprise that the two of them would become friends. There was also Mark, with whom they became close when they were Juniors along with a female named Jade. She was the rider of the bunch. I'd always taken a liking to Laman from a mother's point of view. Jade reminded me of me when I was younger. She was smart and beautiful with a ready-for-whatever mentality. She fit in better around guys than girls. Mark was different. I try to see the good in everyone, but I had my eye on him from the very beginning. His whole character was suspect. They would often hang out, and at first everything was cool. As time passed, Mark started showing signs of jealousy towards Scooby. I don't know if it was just with this one person or if there were others, but it seemed like Scooby was always defending his friends when speaking with him.

In the winter of 2016, he introduced us to a friend named Israel. He and Israel didn't attend the same school but they just so happened to know each other, because they both dated the same girl. Israel dated her first and then later Dasjuan did. They didn't know each other at the time, but later found out when Scooby worked at the barbershop with Tye as a sweeper and Israel came in the shop as a client. Somehow conversation came up, and they realized they had something or should I say someone in common. Her name was Alexandria. The two of them became friends over time. Israel got into a situation where he was given an ultimatum that no teenage kid should have to make. Scooby, having the heart of gold that he has, came to us and asked if we could shelter him. It was customary for Scooby to bring his friends to us who needed temporary shelter. Our hearts would never allow us to turn anyone away as long as they were males. He knew better than to bring a female to us talking about "she needs a place to stay." Yea, that wouldn't end well.

Anyway, we tried to set up a meeting to get the story from his mother's point of view since Israel was a minor. She didn't want to meet with us, so we just met with Israel. I think Israel must have thought we were crazy, because in the midst of our meeting, I received an emergency call from my mom. She thought someone was trying to break into her house.

I said to my husband, "911, we have to go. I'll explain in the car."

I put my tennis shoes on, put my hair back in a ponytail, grabbed my gun, and ran out the door. I was in fearless mode, and I was ready! I don't play about my mother. My husband was right there with me, ready! Luckily for everyone, it was nothing;

we were able to walk away laughing about the incident. I reacted off of pure instinct to protect my mother. My husband reacted off of pure instinct to protect me, because he knew there was no calming me down about that woman.

We got back to the house about an hour and a half later and Israel was still there so we finished the conversation. Talk about a first impression, geesh! We allowed him to move in with us. When Israel moved in, he had no direction. He didn't know what he wanted to do in life; his grades were below average, and he lacked confidence in certain areas. While we were building Israel up, Mark was trying to tear him down by tainting a negative image in Scooby's mind about him. He would tell Scooby that Israel was gay.

He would also say, "I don't like that nigga."

He constantly had something to say about him living with us. He didn't want Scooby near Israel. Scooby said it was because Mark thought he was fragile and couldn't hang with them. I don't even remember them ever meeting.

Scooby also became friends with a guy named Malik. They've known each other since middle school, but Scooby never liked him for whatever reason. Malik is tall, light skinned, with a slender, muscular, and strong build. He liked to slapbox. That's what got Scooby's attention. Scooby has a beautiful dark complexion, beautiful curly hair, and is toothpick skinny with defined muscles. He loved to fight, too. He wouldn't start it, but he welcomed the challenge. When he saw that Malik had fighting hands, he wanted to challenge him. They would go round for round, neither of them giving up. This was how they became friends.

It wasn't long after Scooby developed his circle of friends that I had another vision through a dream. I dreamt that Dasjuan got arrested as a result of him and his friends smoking weed. When I visited him in his cell, I felt an agonizing pain a mother should never feel. He had goals of going into the Air Force after high school.

So in my dream, I said, "Now you've ruined your chances of going into the military."

I woke up and talked to my husband and Dasjuan about this dream. He told me he wasn't smoking weed anymore and had not in a while. I felt relieved.

As Scooby was preparing for graduation, we were trying to find a direction for Israel. We worked on a five year plan. It was a struggle, but we were able to at least get started. He then mentioned that his brother was in the military and that he would consider that. Finally! We were getting somewhere. Report cards came around and now he was an honor roll student. This was a great achievement for him. He said he'd never made the A and B honor roll before. I wish I could have captured the smile on his face and the feeling in his heart after that accomplishment. We felt proud, too, because we were able to help him get there.

Because of his own personal relationship with his parents, Israel then went from calling us Mrs. Aishia and Mr. Tye to Mom and Dad. We took him in as a friend of Scooby's and now he is unofficially adopted into our family. We include him in the count when people ask us how many kids we have.

All of the kids graduated in the same year and around the same time. I really liked Malik. It was something about his mannerisms. I was there cheering on all the kids being the proud momma bear for all of them. I couldn't wait to snap pictures of the new graduates of Frank H. Peterson! The following week was the same way for Israel. He graduated from Westside High. Surprisingly, the only person who showed up from his biological family was his Uncle Dale, who'd been active in his life. That was okay though, because he was happy that he had us there to support him.

August of 2017, my job fired me for no reason. I worked at Tulsa Welding School at the time as a Human Resources Specialist. When I got there at the end of 2015, I had no HR experience other than my eight years of Recruiting and prior relevant work experience. When I came onboard, there was no trust between HR and the employees. I came in and rebuilt the trust between the two offices in Jacksonville. Yes, I made my mistakes. We were able to work past the one I should have been fired for. I started implementing new procedures for the company to make us a healthier, better, more fun place to work.

After about a year, I started noticing some changes in the workplace. Once the Vice President moved to the corporate office, I got this eerie feeling that things were about to go south when he got promoted. But I was still genuinely happy for him. I believe I even spoke about it to one of my Co-workers, Charles. Anyway, I took an early lunch and didn't see where my immediate boss had scheduled a meeting. This upset my boss but I was a salaried employee and didn't have a set time to go to lunch. I didn't understand why she was upset because she was usually the sweetest, most understanding, kindest person I knew. That day, I was talking to a totally different person. Then she asked me if I wanted my job. She started bringing up old stuff that happened when I was first training; on top of little minute things, she also tried to pin things on me that had nothing to do with me. I just listened. I could tell she didn't want to fire me but that she needed to fire someone. She wanted me to fight for my job, I guess, but I was weak. I couldn't fight the tears. I felt betrayed. As I am trying to figure out what was going on with my boss and why this sudden change happened, I can only come to one conclusion. She was highly stressed. It seems that she was in an ethics versus morals battle. It took her three days to come to the conclusion to fire me. I guess ethics superseded her morals but it was all good.

Meanwhile, Dion, the Vice President who was currently in office, didn't want to see me go. He told me to fight, because his hands were tied but I couldn't. I was also talking to my aunt Reba who worked there as well. She and Dion both told me the same thing. They had to remind me that we as black folks were like ants to a giant in the workplace. They said if you don't have a degree, you lose your voice out here. They said, at least with a degree you have a better chance of competing in your fight. These two people were so instrumental with me getting through those miserable three days. On that third day, I was called into the office, and I was fired. Dion was sad for me. I was okay that day though.

Dion hugged me and said he wanted to save me the embarrassment of walking me out. I appreciated that so much. When I got into my car, it felt like a ton of weight was just lifted from my body. I was good. I called my husband and told him what had just occurred.

He said, "God's got it. We're going to be okay."

I streamed David Crowder's song, *How He Loves Me*, and gave God musical praise all the way home. My firing put everyone on notice as people started seeking other employment from what I heard. Before I knew it, I was getting calls about more firings not just from the two Jacksonville offices but the corporate office as well. Time tells all and I was sad for those people. Everyone does not have the family and spiritual support that I have. I was also relieved, because it was confirmation that I wasn't the problem.

Looking for new employment was stressful. It is not like I

wasn't receiving employment opportunities. I just wasn't settling for less than what I was making beforehand. With every job, I have always increased my pay. There was no way I was going to short myself. After a few months, I decided that I will take two dollars less. It seemed like the more I went down on my standards, the more calls I received making less than what I settled for in my mind. Dion and my aunt Reba's words echoed in my head so loudly that I decided to go back to school. I said in my mind, *I'll show them*. I applied to Western Governors University in September and chose Human Resources Management as my major. At that school you had to maintain above a C average, which I most proudly did.

That December, we took Israel to MEPS (Military Entrance Processing Station). That was such an exciting experience to see him feel accomplished. He was like a kid in a candy store when he saw the game room and realized he was about to be on his own. He was nervous too. I was hoping Scooby would be excited at what he saw to get him on the good foot and speed things along, because he was procrastinating with all of his tasks. We found out later that he wanted to wait for a year before he enlisted. Tye and I both tried to get him to understand that a lot could happen in that short timespan; these kids knew everything and nothing.

I remember him telling me, "It's only a year, not too much can happen within that time."

Oh boy, how I wish that were true. It was Thanksgiving of 2017, and Scooby was hanging out with my brother who we found out about while they were in school. It was crazy, because My brother Kumante, my dad's son, was telling his brothers JoJo and Anthony that he has nephews that live in Jacksonville. They then found out that they went to the same school, I guess by way of pictures. Scooby called me furious, because he didn't want it to be true. He said he didn't like the boy, Jojo, who approached him, because he was a showoff. He said Anthony was straight. After Scooby ran down the family history, I confirmed these were his uncles. Scooby had to get off the phone with me to take it all in. He wasn't ready to start a bond with him. He later called me back and told me that he would try. The two of them connected. Scooby told JoJo how he felt, and he accepted it. They moved past differences and began to hang out at clubs since JoJo and Anthony were young promoters and had connections.

On this particular Thanksgiving night, we were at the house watching a football game when suddenly my cell rang. It was the cops. Scooby and Jojo were pulled over in Scooby's car for smoking weed. We immediately left the house and headed to the scene. They had my baby in cuffs and sitting down on the curve. That was hard to see. They had JoJo in the backseat of the police car. The cops were kind, thankfully. Scooby had told them that he had plans to go into the Air Force. When they spoke to us, they wanted confirmation of that. They then asked me his

Sergeant's name. He wanted to make sure it lined up with the name Scooby gave. Because we had the process started already, we were good. They let him go. Unfortunately for JoJo, he wasn't so lucky. He was taken down to the Jacksonville Sheriff's Office because he had an old warrant for a Failure to Appear.

One thing that people tend to forget is that warning always comes before destruction. Case in point, we have specialists who issue public health warnings, warnings about extreme weather conditions, terrorist warnings, etc. God loves us enough to warn us of certain disasters, and it is up to us whether we choose to ignore them. Whether we choose to believe they exist. Whether we are smart enough to take heed. I will say it again: warning comes before destruction.

January rolled around and it was time to drive Israel to Basic Training. The Air Force base was in Lackland, TX. I loved to travel. We did it very often. But that ride was the longest, most boring ride I had ever taken in my life! We took a vow to never, ever drive to Texas again when we saw there was no scenery. I'd rather sit and watch these crazy kid shows that have no substance on Youtube for hours than to take that ride again. The good thing about that trip was that we were able to spend the final moments with youthful Israel. Although he had only been a part of our family for a year, we had grown to love him as a son. Saying goodbye was hard but it was exciting at the same time, because I knew it wasn't the end.

I got into a car accident in January on Martin Luther King's birthday. I was picking up the neighbor's kids from school as a favor, and someone sideswiped my car. This person was clearly high and had just gotten his license back that day. He was shaken, not because of the accident but because he didn't want to lose his license again. Although I was upset about scratches and dings on my car, I sucked it up and provided comfort to this man. I started talking to him about Christ and even invited him to our church. A day later, I started feeling pains in my neck and my lower back, so I went to McGowans Spinal Rehabilitation on Main Street for therapy.

I received treatment from them several times a week until one day, Doctor Royce McGowan said to me, "Aishia, have you considered becoming a Physicians Assistant?"

I told him I hadn't. I asked questions about what they did. He told me that I had the personality of one and then said that I should look into it. I was still studying in my Human Resources classes at this time, but I told him I would research it. I did just that. The more research I did, the more I was drawn to it. I then remembered I had fifty six credits under Allied Health from when I attended Jones College over twenty years ago. This was the direction I began to lean towards. I started thinking about Corporate America and how tired I was of their foolishness. Even though Tulsa Welding School is a private sector, it feels like they are all the same.

As I was working hard to keep my grades up, I was also dealing with the growing pains of a spoiled teenage son. You see, Jabari is as sweet as sugar. He is very respectful. He always keeps me laughing and is an awesome cook. However, my baby boy is very lazy. He has no sense of reality and here is why. As Tye and I were raising him, everything that we did, Jamal would try to undue. When we gave him chores, Jamal would oppose them. I remember Jamal coming to our house for a parent meeting that went south.

As he walked out the door, he looked over to Jabari who was washing dishes then back at us and asked, "Why do y'all have him doing chores? Look at y'alls floors, it's all sparkling clean. Y'all got him working like some slave."

Our floors were tile so of course they were clean. We also had to deal with the fact that when Jabari was making all F's and D's on his report card, his dad was giving him the latest iPhone. I opposed this and for the longest. I told both of them that his iPhone was not coming into our house until those grades came up. Jamal was a great dad but a bad parent. He wanted to be the fun parent.

He loved being dad of the year for show and whenever we got into an argument, he would always say, "My friends can vouch for me for this and that."

However, when his friends weren't around, they couldn't see all of the mental poison he was feeding Jabari. I could write a full book about this poison, but I'm not here to bash Jamal. It's just that seventeen years of going against our rational teachings is the reason we battled laziness in Jabari. It was exhausting battling my son, and dealing with his father who took me to court on child abuse and neglect allegations. I wasn't even upset at that mendacious propaganda. It was a new low for him. I was more shocked than anything. As a matter of fact, the mediator asked me if I felt comfortable with him having two lawyers and I not having any present.

  I responded, "My lawyer is present, you just can't see him."

  I refused to waste money on a lawyer when it was obvious that he had no grounds for his claims. I love my kids. Anyone could recognize that. I chose to spend retainer money on something more valuable: my family.

  Before we went into court my husband said, "Bend, don't break."

  He was reminding me that I am a Christian so I need to have leniency with sharing time, but don't overdo it to where I will regret it. When they asked about the parenting plan, I gave him all the time he asked for. I even opted not to put him on child support despite the evil done to me. The one thing I did not do was allow him to claim Jabari on his taxes anymore. That killed him. Every year we were supposed to split the taxes and every year it was always a sob story. The last time it was about his grandmother dying, and he needed to go to New York. I called his twin sister, Jamila, to confirm. Of course, it was not true. I had never fallen for his sob stories but had allowed him to cheat me with the taxes, because you will never catch me arguing over money. I don't care how bad my situation is, I refuse to do it. So yes, I got control of the tax situation and gave him another reason to hate me. Every tax season, I knew it was going to be drama, and it was. I had gotten to a point where I allowed myself to become a piñata for the sake of Jabari. I didn't want him to see his parents feuding back and forth. You see, I couldn't control his actions, but I could control mine. And that is what I did. Once every blue moon, I'd remind him that I choose to take his mess. For the most part, I realized that if I wasn't arguing with my husband, I surely wasn't going to give him the satisfaction. It's funny because when I gave in, I was convicted by the Holy Spirit. He'd prick my heart, and I'd feel this conviction to remind me that I was doing wrong. Sometimes I'd call Jamal back and apologize for my actions, because I knew better than to retaliate verbally. But I can't say it did not bother me to always be the bigger person. I just didn't allow it to bother me for long. During this time, I was also fighting to maintain my 3.5 GPA at Western Governors University, while also having to stay on Jabari for his grades. I literally had to stand over him to make sure he got his homework done. I stayed on top of TJ as well as his homework and sports activities. To add to the madness, Scooby moved out of the house. This was a slap in the face, because we wanted to help him find a place to stay. He was so anxious to be out on his own, he left to go stay with friends.

I reminded him of my dream, and he assured me that he would be okay. Something was off though. The way he left was just all wrong, but he was eighteen. He had his diploma, so we couldn't hold him back. We didn't agree but still supported his decision. When he left, he went to live with some female friends. He learned quickly that the grass isn't greener on the other side. He wanted to come back, but pride wouldn't let him. After about two or three months, he ended up moving into his own place with Jade. He was gone a total of six months before he came back home. Within those six months, he was shot at twice, robbed and was going back and forth with his friend Mark about foolishness.

My grade in one of my classes dropped from a B average to a D average. No matter how hard I tried, I couldn't recover that grade. My husband told me that some of these issues I couldn't control. The one thing that he wouldn't allow me to do any more was to stand over Jabari to make sure he was doing what he was supposed to. He said that was one stress that could be eliminated. He was right.

It was also at that point where I decided to change my career choice. I decided to major in Health Sciences. Western Governors University didn't have a Health Sciences program, so I transferred to Purdue Global University. A wavering path reduces your ability to think properly and effectively. This was why I promised that no matter what, I would not allow anything to disrupt the path I set for myself.

When God gives us visions, we never know when it's coming to fruition. Evidently, going back to school was in His Will. Apparently, it wasn't for me to be at WGU. He had a path for me but I needed to be patient to see what it was. Patience is key. Just like when he gave me the dream about Scooby going to jail when he was still an innocent soul, it took six years for it to be fulfilled. When he gave me the dream about Scooby going to jail he was still an innocent soul. Now at twenty years old, he started exploring a new religion. It was called Pythagoreansim. He wasn't sure what it was called, but his uncle and my sister believed in it and it captured his interest. All I know is that he kept talking about triangles and numbers. I googled it and that is what I came up with. It was not long after finding this religion that things went dark.

Mark and Scooby got into a huge argument, because Mark knew that Scooby's girl had cheated on him with their friend Laman and didn't tell Scooby. Scooby felt betrayed, because, not only did he not tell him but, he allowed it to happen in his house. Scooby said that was the last straw with Mark. He was seeing too many shady things with him and he's too loyal to be around someone who he can't trust. He eventually forgave Laman because he came clean about it and apologized. I'll never forget the day he came home hurt.

I provided him comfort, and then we got into the discussion of breaking cycles. He and I were always getting into deep discussions. I believe this one started, because he was trying to understand the actions of the girl he was about to end his long term relationship with. He knew I had been raped and molested. Unfortunately, he had also been sexually abused by a family member. The conversation got really deep. When the family member violated him, he was staying the night with them. It was another child who did it. He reminded me of his feelings during that time. When I found out about what happened, I was furious! This brought back painful memories from my past, but most importantly, this was my son! I was prepared to go into full assassin mode on any violator to any loved one, but this was a child. I wasn't prepared to handle this so, with understanding her age and curiosity, I talked with her in hopes this would be the first and last time. I didn't let my son spend the night over again but I did allow the adult to babysit again thinking that the child was remorseful enough to act like a child again.

Unfortunately, it didn't stop there. The next time he went over there, I remember receiving a call from work from Dasjuan. He was crying and pleading with me, telling me to hurry up and come get him. He said that she was grabbing him as he was holding onto the walls. As he was crying, he was telling her no, but she kept begging him and pulling on his waist. He told her to leave him alone. I left work that day and grabbed my baby. I had all kinds of evil thoughts running through my head at that time, but the first thing I wanted to do was to hug my son. Needless to say, he never went over there again without me.

As we were speaking, he said he needed to call that family member to ask them about what happened. He needed to make peace with the situation for his own sake. He said someone needed to break the cycle, and it was going to start with him. He chose to forgive. We finished talking so that he could go make the call he needed. Later in the evening he told me he had gotten the apology that he was looking for. Then, something happened.

I noticed a slight shift in Scooby's demeanor that only a mother or an old school grandmother would notice. We were standing in the kitchen by the pantry door. I asked if he was okay.

He said, "Yes ma'am."

Then he leaned over the counter and I asked, "Scooby, what's going on?"

That's when he told me that his back was hurting him really bad. I rubbed his back, and it felt as if his spine was misaligned. It shifted and bulged slightly. It was weird. I gave him a back brace to use. I also advised him to make an appointment to see Dr. McGowan. I told him he would get him fixed up. I asked if he wanted Motrin. He took it and laid down for a few. He got up later that evening and said that he felt better. He wanted to go see Mark. He was going to apologize to him even though the argument wasn't his fault.

He said, "I no longer want to be his friend, I just want peace. I'm all about having peace in my life, Mom. That's where I'm at. I'm not with this drama. So if I have to apologize for something that is not my fault just for peace, I'll do that."

I told him to be careful. I reminded him that I didn't trust Mark, but he said he would be fine and headed out the door. From this point on, things got choppy and blurry. Bear with me as I try to tell this story the best as I can, because so much poison was placed in this body at once that it caused a supernatural explosion.

Scooby arrived at Mark's place to discuss what went down. They sat in the car to talk about what happened. Scooby apologized for whatever Mark thought Scooby did wrong. Mark then apologized to Scooby for betraying him, and then they fired one up. There's an old saying that goes, "Keep your enemies close and your friends closer." Here's why.

I don't know if this was intentional or unintentional, but the weed that they smoked that night was laced. There was a possibility that it was unintentional, because people reach for that new high all the time. And sometimes, they wouldn't tell their smoke partners maybe out of embarrassment or fear. I can't call what was in Mark's heart that night, and it's not like he is honorable enough to tell me. What I do know is the effect that it had on our son and how our Christianity was challenged for a week straight. The first sign that something was wrong was that Scooby denounced Christ. He started talking about those triangles and numbers that other family members were feeding him. My heart was breaking. I couldn't understand what was happening to my son. His family members who practiced these same beliefs were teaching him to have outer body experiences and how to tap into different dimensions.

Scooby has always been super smart. His favorite subject was science, so of course this was appealing to him. He would talk to Tye and tell him that this was the way that Jesus wanted him to get to everlasting life. He would also talk about how he was one with nature. I heard people talking like that all the time, but this was different.

My son told me he was a god. We went back and forth, because I wanted to keep him talking so I could understand what was going on with him.

This way I would know how to help him, but then he said, "I can walk on water."

I realized then that I was talking to a total stranger. I knew his eyes seemed a bit different, but this guy had my son's vessel. Why would I think otherwise?

I asked "Who am I talking to right now?

He said, "What?"

I was like, *Mmhm*. I was done with this conversation and I walked off. I was confused. I needed to gather my thoughts.

Scooby went home and started drawing symbols of triangles on a white sheet of paper. It also had some numbers on it. He tried to explain it to me. It made absolutely no sense because at this point I had shut down a listening ear to Scooby's irrational talk.

As Proverbs 26:5 says, "If you answer a fool according to his folly, he will be wise in his own eyes."

I wasn't trying to feed into his foolishness any longer. I'd had enough of trying to understand him. At this point, he needed to understand me and my husband. We are a Christian household who believed that Jesus Christ is our Lord and Savior. There is no other way to get to God except through him! Your grandma's relationship can't save you; no affiliations can save you; no social status, race or religion can save you. Only your own personal relationship with Jesus will save you. We also needed him to understand that Jabari and TJ were still in our house, and they didn't need to listen to his misguided foolishness. The sad part about it was he was bringing people with him with his beliefs.

Malik was so loyal to Scooby that he'd follow him wherever he'd go. Malik was one who came and stayed with us for quite some time even after Scooby moved out. When he was with us, Scooby was telling him about Christ. When Scooby started practicing this religion, he brought Malik and others in on this as well. This is dangerous, because by the time you find out that it's actually not the way to go, you may have gotten someone in so deep that they can't get out. If you are practicing something that people may look at as crazy, you may want to avoid it, it's that simple.

Day three, Scooby woke up and appeared to be fine. He told me that he was going to my nephew, Jah'mal's house. This was nothing out of the ordinary. It was around eleven in the morning when I was straightening my hair. Jabari had a show downtown. He is a talented rap artist. I never made it to his previous shows; I told him that he will always have my support, but I supported education over rapping. I told him that he will see me when he starts to bring his grades up.

During this time, his grades were better, and I was excited to finally catch one of his rap shows. Suddenly, I received a call from Jah'mal's girlfriend, Keke.

She said, "Something is wrong with Dada [That was another childhood name for Dasjuan given to him by Jah'mal]."

She continued, "He's acting really strange. He's around here playing with my daughter outside with no shoes on."

Her daughter at the time was young, between eight or nine years old.

She said, "Jah'mal thinks he's just high but auntie, something is seriously wrong with him."

Then she mentioned something really strange that made me reflect on the prior days' behaviors. She told me they were playing with their blood in the dirt. I was disturbed! I often wondered why she didn't go and grab her daughter, but she has been in the family for so long, I guess she didn't want to agitate him for the safety of her daughter. At the same time, she trusted that he wouldn't hurt her. She did keep her eye on them until I got there.

I dropped everything and immediately went to their house. I called Jabari on the way and apologized that I wouldn't be able to make it. He was looking forward to me being there, but he understood. I didn't tell him exactly what was going on, but I told him I received an emergency call about Scooby. I assured him that he would be okay and to focus on his performance. When I got there Scooby and the little girl were in the backyard of the apartments at the park, which my niece could see from their apartment window.

When I saw him, he was on the slides. Her daughter was having the best of fun playing with him.

I called his name, "Dasjuan."

"Oh, hey Momma," he said with a smile.

He then walked over to me barefoot.

I asked, "Where are your shoes?"

I can't tell you his response because during this time, our conversations were a mix of intelligence and unintelligible gibberish. One minute he would answer my questions, the next he was talking about triangles and numbers. I looked into his eyes; at times I wasn't seeing my son. I felt like I was dealing with multiple people.

I said, "Baby, something is wrong with you."

He said, "I know."

"We need to go get you evaluated."

He said okay but then said, "But Ma, wait…"

He started talking about triangles and numbers again. I'd tell him I heard him, but we needed to get him to the hospital.

We would walk a little further and he said again, "Mom, wait, I know I need help but check out these triangles."

He would pull out that white piece of paper that he drew a few days ago and would try to explain. With every couple of steps, he would continue to stall until we finally got to the car.

I got him in and locked the door. I strapped the seatbelt around him from the driver's side, and we headed straight to the hospital. I told him that I didn't want to hear anything else about no daggone triangles. As we were en route to the hospital, I explained again that I was going to have him evaluated. He asked me if they were going to admit him.

I said, "Look, right now you are showing signs of being mentally unstable. Things seem to be getting progressively worse. If they feel that you are a threat to yourself or someone else, they will keep you. But right now, let's focus on finding out what happened to you."

As this was going on, I was trying to remain strong. It was hard seeing my firstborn in this way. He was so loving and full of life and suddenly, it appeared that he had a mental illness.

How long will this last? How did we get here? I asked myself. *Lord, I need your strength, because I can't do this on my own*, I quickly prayed. Next, I called my husband to fill him in on all the details and let him know I was taking Scooby to Baptist Hospital on Prudential Drive. He asked if I wanted him to leave work. I told him to finish up with his clients first. He said to call him if I needed him. Walking up to the hospital, Scooby continued with the stall tactics.

We eventually made it inside. I told the Patient Service Representative at the desk that I believed my son had gotten his hands on some bad weed.

"I need him to be checked out immediately!" I urged.

They identified him and immediately took him to triage. After triage, he was taken to another room where he had to take a drug test.

I couldn't go into that room. It was there where I broke down. There was a white lady sitting there, I call her my angel. I didn't see her at first, but she saw me.

She said, "Ma'am, I don't know what you're going through but I see that you are hurting."

She told me everything will be okay. She said God is in control, and she hugged me. She left me her number, and I held onto it for a long time. I wanted to reach out to her to thank her and tell her how much I needed her at that moment. I never did. Then one day, I couldn't find her number anymore. But this lady, who was there for her son's broken arm, had taken the time out to comfort me; A total stranger. Let that sink in.

We were then taken to our room. As we were waiting on the doctor to come in and read the results, the Certified Nurse Assistant came in to check on Scooby. He asked her if he could touch her hand. Weird! My son would have never done that. She of course said no. He also put his head under the white sheets and told me that he had died and came back. My heart was breaking with every moment, but I was holding it together. Malik and his girlfriend Moriah got word about Scooby and came to visit him. Malik was upset! Whatever Scooby had gotten into, he was waiting for him to get better so that they could throw hands. Scooby knew better, and Malik was going to hold him accountable for being stupid.

The doctor finally came in and called me out of the room.

"Mrs. McQuillan, your son has Flakka in his system."

"What is Flakka?" I asked.

He responded, "It's a synthetic drug that is compared to cocaine, but is ten times worse. Its effects are similar to those of bath salts."

I grabbed my face as my hands slid down my head. My heart was pounding so hard that the doctor probably heard it.

"It was just last year or maybe the year prior where there was news coverage about people in Miami taking bath salts. It was having a zombie-like effect on them, and they had superhuman strength, right?"

He said, "Yes, unfortunately. We have two choices. We need to Baker Act him. We can either take him voluntarily or involuntarily. This means if he goes with us, he will only have to stay for three nights, if all goes well. If he refuses to go then we will have to take him away from this hospital and lock him away at another hospital. And you don't want that. He has more freedom at this one."

"Why does he need to be taken away?" I asked.

I had so many emotions going at once that I couldn't capture them all. All I knew was, I didn't want my baby out of my sight. I needed to protect him whether from himself or others. My son needed me. *How could I protect him if he's out of my sight? He's not himself*, I thought

The doctor continued, "Once they start coming down off of this, he may pose a threat to himself or others. He needs to be supervised."

I said, "But my son is a loveable being. He doesn't want to hurt anyone."

The doctor said "Ma'am, trust me. We are looking out for his best interests here. We know that it is not him personally, rather the drug in his system that is in control. I've seen many instances of this, and it never ends well."

I asked about his mental health after this. Hopefully, this won't create permanent mental damage.

"With Flakka, it can go either way," he continued, "If this was his first time, he has a shot of going back to being normal."

I cried. I held it together, but I cried. I called my husband and updated him on what was going on. Davida, one of the young sisters from our church, was getting baptised that Sunday. I was scheduled for Deaconess duties. I called Tanisha, the Pastor's wife, to let her know that I wasn't going to make it. I tried to hold in the tears. Tanisha is also my friend, so she knew immediately that something was wrong. I told her I would be okay. It had to have been the Holy Spirit that touched Tanisha in that moment, because she immediately went into prayer with me. It was the prayer I needed. I broke down again. I was safe with her so I filled her in briefly after the prayer and told her I would call her later to fill her in with the rest. Little did she know, her prayer uplifted me and gave me the strength I needed to get through the rest of the night.

After I got off the phone with Tanisha, I had called the family and filled them in. I am not big on telling people what's going on with me. I forced myself to reach out to Antoine. He's Scooby's biological father, so I had the responsibility to fill him in. Then I sent a group text to my Jacksonville siblings. Mom was called in the car when I was on my way to the hospital. If I was going to tell someone something -someone other than Tye- she would be the first to know.

Scooby's immediate family came to see him that night.

I found out that while he was at the hospital, two of his family members said to him, "People are going to think you're crazy, but you're not crazy. It's them."

Luckily, I didn't find that out that night.

All I could think of was Matthew 7:15, "Beware of false prophets who come to you in sheep's clothing, but inwardly are ravenous wolves."

These people, who were supposed to love my son, who I trusted, and who he trusted saw my son at his lowest point. And this was a victory for them. How sick! I didn't even want to speak on what could have happened had we found out what was said that night.

Mom couldn't come that night because she and Dot were watching TJ for us. Everyone else came to support or erode which I found out later. They took turns to see him and then left. Me, Tye, Malik and Moriah stayed with him until the nurses came in to take him away. When Malik found out the weed was laced with Flakka, he was ready for war. As a matter of fact, Dasjuan's paternal side was planning for war. Scooby was asking them to forgive Mark. The mother in me wanted to be ready for war with them, but the Christan in me had to do things the right way. I have to remember that no matter how tough a situation may get, God is still in control. I had to have enough faith to allow him to control this situation as well. I've been low before, but I had never in my life been dragged down this low. I was sitting there watching my son switch between different personalities, not knowing how many there were. I wasn't about to count them. I just wanted them to go away. I wanted my son back!

The nurse finally came in with a wheelchair to take him away. I looked at him with pain in my eyes as he hopped from the bed to the wheelchair.

He said, "I'm going to be okay, Momma."

I smiled. Suddenly, there was another change as he was headed out the door. The being that was using my son's body looked at me and licked his tongue at me in a playful manner. My son would normally do that to get me to smile. However, when I looked into his eyes, those weren't my son's eyes. I repeated my thoughts to my husband as he was being wheeled away.

He asked, "What do you mean?"

"I know my son. Those were not his eyes."

I have never seen my son act in any supernatural way before, but with Flakka in his system, it appeared that he had been possessed by something. I'd heard stories of other family members being attacked violently by demons when they were high on drugs. I'd also heard stories of demons haunting certain houses up north that belonged to my family, but I had no reason to believe that I was dealing with evil. I only knew I wasn't dealing with the son I had raised for the last twenty years.

That night, I refused to leave the hospital. I was going to stay close to my baby even though I couldn't physically be in the room with him. I was adamant about sleeping in the parking garage, but my husband wouldn't let me. I didn't want to leave. I wanted him to feel my presence there somehow, some way. That night I called to check on him. The Mental Health Nurse who answered the phone wouldn't give me any info, because the doctor forgot to give me a code. I had to plead with her as a mother. She still refused. I called back and told them that I would keep calling back until I got answers, because I just wanted to make sure my son was okay.

The nurse finally said "If your son is here, he is doing okay. You can come and see him tomorrow, *if he is here.*"

I was fine with that. The day was exhausting and after my long hot shower, I slept in my husband's arms all night. That next morning, February 16th, I was up by 7:00 a.m. I called to check on Dasjuan and to let them know I would come early to get the code. My heart broke instantly! Tears ran down my face. My husband asked what was wrong.

The male mental health nurse had just told me that we couldn't go and see Scooby.

He said, "Around midnight Scooby leaped over the desk, attacked two females, and was going after another until myself and another male nurse had to hold him down. Scooby had Superhuman-like strength. These desks stand pretty high and he leaped over it with no hands. He even tried to run through the glass a couple of times. We don't like to sedate our patients, but we eventually had to for our own safety and his."

He paused before continuing, "He seems like a good kid. I hope he overcomes whatever he's going through."

Then he told me to try again tomorrow.

Tye was hurt. I was devastated. I told him I was going down there anyway.

He said, "For what, they won't let you see him?"

I repeated myself, "I'm going to see my son."

He told me to call my mom, since she was looking forward to going to see him. I broke the news to her, too. I told her that I was going down to the hospital. She said she would meet me there. I walked in and tried to see him. They wouldn't allow me to. I was in no condition to fight. I was mentally weak and physically drained. I walked outside and sat on the bench waiting for Mom. I knew she was coming to my rescue and would be dressed to perfection doing it.

As I sat on the bench waiting, I received a call from Charles, "Hey sis!"

"Hey bro!" I started bawling! "I can't talk right now. Tell Madi happy birthday."

I didn't realize it wasn't my niece's birthday. I was a few days early. I didn't realize until I started writing this book that it was another niece's birthday. I sat in pause for a long time before I wrote these next two lines.

It was the birthday of the niece who violated Scooby. I

just saw life in reverse and was able to connect the dots. The demon began to manifest itself in Scooby's body when my niece apologized to him. It took full control on her birthday. Of course there were other factors involved that assisted in opening the gateway, but obviously there is some significance. Two years later, I am in total shock!

So I filled my brother in on what was going on with Scooby. He explained that he went through something similar with another nephew's weed being laced and told me he came out fine. He provided me with brotherly comfort and then told me to keep him posted. Mom and Dot pulled up, and we got off the phone. Just as I thought, she came dressed just as prissy as she could be, ready to protect and defend. I told her they wouldn't let me see him.

She said, "Come on."

I straightened my face. With Mom by my side, I felt stronger. Mom and I don't see eye to eye spiritually, but she is my strength when I am weak. I am the same for her when she needs it. She went to the same receptionist I went to and told them that we never received a code. She introduced herself as Dajuan's grandmother and me as his mother. She told them she understands that they wouldn't give us info without a code but that we needed to speak with someone who would give us information. She was sweet and stern, but her presence was felt.

Next thing I knew, the lady was sending us upstairs to the

Psych Unit. A female nurse came down to greet us. She said that she couldn't guarantee that we would see my son but wanted to provide us with answers. We walked down a long floor as we talked about what happened. Then we went down another set of long corridors until we reached the elevators. From there, we arrived on the floor where the mental patients were. We walked down another set of long white halls until we reached the outside. I believed that door led to another door where we were greeted by a half-gated receptionist entry. The mental health nurse pretty much reiterated everything the male nurse had told us.

When my mom asked how the women were, she replied, "He ripped one of the ladies' earrings out of her ear. She is downstairs being treated at the hospital. She quit this morning. The other lady has minor injuries."

I cried some more. I felt deep compassion for those ladies. My son does not act like that. He protects women; he does not hurt them. I guess this was what the doctor meant when he said Scooby could be a danger to himself or others when he comes down off of it. Mom asked if we could see him. She said if he is awake then she will let us see him. She told us that we would have to leave our phones and purses in the lockers outside. We were okay with that. We were hopeful at the opportunity to see Scooby.

Mom hugged me tightly, rubbing her comforting arms down my back until the nurse returned.

She came back and said, "Unfortunately, he is still sedated. Try back later today around seven. We will allow you to see him."

I walked away feeling that we had accomplished something today that I couldn't have done without Mom's help. When we got back downstairs, Dot, who stayed in the car, told me I was in no condition to drive. She volunteered to drive my car back to my house and meet us there. I thanked my mom for being there, and we headed home. I couldn't wait to tell Tye the good news.

Later that evening, Tye and I headed to the hospital. We were there on time. Scooby was coming out of sedation. I laid on the hospital bed where he was and just held my baby. I examined his body; once again, I was heartbroken. My baby looked worn. His fingernails were cut short and filled with dry blood around the nail bed. There were minor scratches on his body. When we asked what happened, the male nurse first got onto me about being on his bed. He said we weren't supposed to be that close to him. But that was my baby. He wasn't going to hurt me, but I knew I had to follow the rules.

He repeated the story of what happened again. He said those wounds were self-inflicted. He also said one of the women who got hurt was talking about filing a lawsuit against Scooby. He said he wouldn't be too concerned about that though. This guy seemed to like Scooby.

My son noticed us as he was in and out of sedation. He smiled. We stayed there until he came to. His eyes were opening and shutting as he was talking, but he told us that there was a lady there who was an angel. He said she has a family, but they don't know that she is there. He asked me if I could help her find her loved ones. That's just like Scooby putting other people before him. I told him that I would, and I actually took a few minutes to google search and look for them on Facebook. I don't remember any of their names now, but I did what my son asked me to do. During our visit, he then started talking about the triangles again. We told him that if he wanted to get out of there, he needed to shut up about those triangles and leave them alone. We visited him each day they would allow. He called on the fourth day telling us he was coming home. The first thing he wanted to do before he got in the car was to stand by the ledge of the parking garage for some fresh air. This scared me knowing he had made an attempt to jump through glass while he was in the ward, but I had to trust that he was better. I was prepared to grab him if he wasn't. Thankfully, he really did just want fresh air, and I understood why. That place didn't have a pleasant smell.

When he came home, the boys were excited. They were in Jabari's room worshipping God by singing J. Moss' song *God's Got It*. Suddenly, there was a hard knock at the door.

"J.S.O. Open up."

It was the Jacksonville Sheriff's Office coming to arrest Scooby for attacking the nurses. I explained the situation to the police.

He said to me, "I'm sorry ma'am. I really am, but there is nothing I can do because she filed charges."

Will this nightmare ever end? I thought. The police came and arrested Scooby.

Tye and I were in our bedroom comforting TJ when suddenly I gasped, "Bae! Do you remember the dream I had a couple of years ago about Scooby getting arrested when I said, 'Now you've ruined your chances of getting into the military.'?"

We all just stared at each other because even TJ remembered me reminding him to take heed of the warnings from my dream. Remember when I said warning comes before destruction? God had given Scooby several warnings that he didn't take heed of; here we were, watching another prophetic dream come true.

The next morning we called our Pastor. He met us down at the jail for support. We also went to Make It Happen Bail Bonds and were able to bail him out. I then called Tanisha and updated her on Scooby. Afterall, she loves Scooby dearly and the feelings are mutual with him. This was a big thing for me, because I am a private person and don't let anyone in my business like this. But Ingrid is a friend of mine from church and is also Tyrone's wife; he was the one who referred us to the church. She told me long before this incident that sometimes I need to let people know what is going on with me so they can pray for me. I told her then that people could just keep me in prayer. She said sometimes, a person needs to pray specific prayers and everyone needs someone to talk to. She was very sincere.

From that point on I started opening up to very few people. Ingrid is one, but Tanisha is another.

When I called Tanisha and filled her in as I promised, she said, "You have to fight the supernatural with the supernatural. We are going to go into fasting. You guys aren't alone. I will fast every day with you for as long as I need to. We will fast, pray, and I will send you scriptures that we can go over."

I cried. I have had great friends. My friends have given me great advice over the years and have been there for me through thick and thin. Now, I was dealing with the supernatural.

There was only one who said, "I am in this with you."

Those words touched me to the core! I am grateful for those who were there for me during those times, and I am indebted to Tanisha for being my hero. She stuck to her word.

The day seemed normal when Scooby first got out of jail. He told us Satan was trying to attack him, but that was it. We were conversing as normal, and then he told me about the secret conversation that happened in the hospital with his family members about everyone else being crazy. I contacted one of those betrayers. I could tell in retrospect that the Pastor, his

Pastor's wife, the Reverend, and his wife were praying for us. They were the only people who knew what was happening outside of the immediate family. I had a sense of calm about me throughout the whole conversation. This person had the audacity to tell me that this evil (although they didn't use the word evil) was for everyone. I knew exactly what I was dealing with. I was quickly reminded that, *"We don't wrestle against flesh and blood but against principalities, against powers and against the rulers of darkness of this world and spiritual wickedness in high places."*

I refused to even give into the ignorance.

I said, "We are trying to raise him in a Christian household. Leave him out of this foolishness!"

This person tried to convince me that Scooby was coming to them for information, but I was not trying to hear it. This person is family and should've had enough love for him to discourage his curiosities.

We arrived home; some time went by. He was acting a bit weird, but he tried to cover it up. I kept telling him he was making me nervous. I begged him to not make me have to take him back. I hated that place for him, but I needed to get him help before he hurt someone. I told him I had other kids in the house to protect and that I would not allow him to traumatize them. He told me he wasn't going back to that place.

February 21st, 2019 was Jabari's birthday. Those split personalities came back. Not only that, but Scooby was showing signs of demonic possession. He would make strange sounds in his breathing. He would cry all the time. He had a body odor which was strange, because Scooby usually bathed daily. However, during this week, he didn't want to. Malik and Moriah came by to check on Scooby. The spirit was uncomfortable around me, but he was comfortable with them. He took a liking to Moriah. Malik had had enough with Scooby and his split personalities, so he told him to step outside. He wanted to beat it out of him. It had nothing to do with Moriah because it wasn't being disrespectful towards her. It was that the whole situation was too much to bear. Malik wanted his brother back. It brought Malik to tears.

I had to remind Malik that his brother was still inside. I told him not to feed into that demonic spirit, because that was what it wanted. It challenged Malik anyway. They took it outside. I had Moriah call Tye and have him get home immediately.

I looked that demon in the eye and said, "Satan, you cannot have my son. My God is bigger and stronger than yours will ever be, and we will win this war."

Malik was still in the mindset that, "I will put you down if I have to."

His position was that there were two females here that he loved and had to protect no matter what. While Malik was in position along with Scooby, I was trying to keep them from fighting. Malik wouldn't have hurt Scooby, but I still took the precaution. I was also on standby, prepared to subdue my baby if things got out of control before Tye got there. Finally, he pulled up in the driveway, but he didn't see us initially. He went into the house and called my name, but we were outside by the pond.

When he walked around the back Scooby pointed at Tye and said, "Not even this guy."

This voice wasn't Scooby's. It stopped Tye in his tracks. It threw him off guard. It took a minute to register that this was a serious situation. The demon in Scooby's body started saying some off the wall stuff. Neither Tye nor I can remember what he was saying, but it was threatening us.

The next thing I know, Tye grabbed him and started praying immediately.

He just started calling on the Lord, "Jesus, Jesus, Jesus!"

We all joined in, "Jesus, Jesus, Jesus!"

Then Moriah said that she had some holy oil in the car. She ran to grab it. We put it on his forehead and prayed for God to remove the demon away from his body and far away from our house. After that prayer, we continued to call on Jesus. Hours went by. It was two thirty, and I had to pick TJ up from school. I called his godparents, told them we'd had an emergency, and asked if I could bring him by for a few hours. They happily agreed. I laughed with him and talked about his day like nothing was going on. That's when my acting skills kicked in, and it worked. TJ suspected nothing. I remembered Jabari was going straight to his dad's, so I didn't have to worry about him until later that evening. I was hoping this would be over by then.

When I came back from dropping TJ off, I saw that Tye had Scooby pinned up against the wall. He was looking for answers.

"Who are you?" I heard him ask.

"Dasjuan," the demon said.

Tye wasn't buying it.

He knew this wasn't his son. He asked again, and again, and again until finally, the demon said, "Dada."

I gasped. As I explained earlier, Dada was a childhood name given to Scooby by my nephew Jah'mal. My nieces and nephews from Tot are the only ones who call him by that name. The demon must have gravitated to that name, but to this day, I hate it when they call him that. Something happened in that moment that made Tye have to put Dasjuan down again.

Those personalities were coming out again. Our son was trying to come out, too. When it was Dasjuan, he was asking Malik to forgive him. He was also telling us that he didn't want to let the demon go. He said he's had him since he was a child and that it had been protecting him. This brought me back to my mom telling me when Scooby was younger that he had a dark side. I didn't believe her. My Scooby was sweet. He'd never given me any trouble. He'd always been an honor roll student up until he finished school. He was even in the National Honor Society.

I didn't see what she saw.

Tye even said to me one time that, "If anyone ever makes Scooby mad and that darkside comes out, I feel sorry for them."

They were the only two that saw it. Actually, there was this incident after Scooby had smoked weed for the first time. He started convulsing and foaming out of the mouth. He was getting a bit wild, so Tye held him down to calm him down. When Tye let him up, Scooby bolted out the door. We drove around and caught up with him then took him to the hospital. We were told that he was dehydrated and that's what we believed then. I didn't not see what Tye and Mom saw. Now looking at things in retrospect, that weed was a gateway for the supernatural. But, anyway, as he was going in and out of his personalities. He continued to tell me that his cousin hurt him. Then he shocked me by saying he didn't think I did enough to protect him. I told him I did what I knew how to do. I explained that they were both children. I couldn't put a child in jail.

I told him when I asked my mom for advice, she told me that that's what kids do. I shared with him how I fussed at my own mother for that comment and didn't call her for a while, because I was tired of hearing those words.

I said, "I also removed you from that situation. If you think back to that incident, you will see that you never went there again after that without me. If it were someone just a bit older, I would've known exactly what to do. But it was me and you against the world. I had absolutely no one to help me through mine, so I had to do the best I knew how with you."

He said, "I wish I knew that then."

"We've always been able to talk about everything since day one. You should have come to me."

Then Scooby asked Malik -as he'd done several times within these hours that he was being held down- if he forgave Mark.

Malik kept saying, "I can't."

Scooby said, "I need you too."

Then those other personalities intervened, similar to the movie *Split* where he'd go from being childlike, to constantly crying, to actually being himself .

We went back to calling Jesus and praying. I looked at Malik, and even he was praying. This was different for Malik. I couldn't believe my eyes. I was literally watching a spiritual battle right before my eyes! Scooby would come back through.

He asked Malik if he forgave Mark, and finally, Malik said, "Yes."

Scooby smiled. Suddenly, the demon became crafty by pretending to be Scooby. He tried to convince us that he felt better. We asked him several times. Of course we felt bad for Scooby because we literally had him pinned down for hours. He stood him up. Everyone was on guard. I looked at Scooby in his eyes, and they shifted like an alien's. I guess that is the best way to describe it.

I think it scared Scooby too, because just as quickly, I said, "That's not Scooby, put him down!"

Scooby said, "Put me back down!"

He told us that he didn't want to hold onto that demon anymore.

We told him to let it go! We told him to profess Christ as his Lord and Savior. It probably took about another hour or so for it to be completely gone. Then when it left, we hugged and hugged and hugged. Nine consecutive days of pure hell on earth, and we finally felt relief. God gave us victory!

Dasjuan's color came back to him. His eyes belonged to him again. I immediately touched his spine, and it was back in alignment. Our son was back! So we thought.

As far as the demon, yes, it was gone. But as far as the son we once knew, we may never have him back. The Scooby before the Flakka was full of life and determination. The Scooby after Flakka seemed more paranoid about everything, not as happy, and was clearly struggling for peace.

This is why it is so important for us to take heed to God's warnings. Because God cannot lie; it's impossible for Him. There was one part of the dream that I noticed hadn't come true as of yet. I kept reminding Scooby that I still hadn't said those words, "Now you have ruined your chances of going into the military."

Once we bailed Scooby out, we got an attorney who reduced his felony charge to a misdemeanor. So, although he missed out on getting into the Air Force, he still had a chance of going into the Navy. He told me that he wouldn't get into any more trouble. He moved out of my house again and started a family. The week that he moved out, he had let his anger get the best of him. He punched through glass and severed a main artery in his right arm. He had lost a lot of tissue and they had to reconstruct his arm using a cadaver graft. The wound was so big they had to figure out how to close it. He had lost mobility in his arm to the point where I looked at him and he already knew what I was thinking, because I kept warning him. He even mentioned to my dad that I was going to tell him that and how he was sad that he disappointed me. That's why I chose not to mention it, but he knew, and the full prophecy had been fulfilled.

Warning comes before destruction. Once again, you can choose to take heed or choose to ignore. Ignoring doesn't change the outcome. It just makes you ignorant to the facts. If you take heed and you are in God, you have victory. Period. Not because we deserve it but because of God's grace and mercy.

I was still in school during this time. I didn't miss one assignment, nor did my grades drop. My spirit was weak and defeated, but God's Holy Spirit stepped in and gave me the strength to get the job done. During this time, I learnt what it truly meant to be patient and cast all your burdens on God. Being a Christian doesn't mean you won't get tested, and you can't put your Christianity down when you're struggling and then pick it back up when you're finished acting like the rest of the world.

We were tested in the worst spiritual way possible, but God put people in our place to get us through it. We just had to remain faithful and let God do the work.

GOD'S WILL

It was the summer of 2019. I had just received a phone call that my niece had gotten into some trouble with the law and that her kids were being moved into different homes until things got straightened out. My niece, Jia, rightfully cared more about where her five children were being placed than fighting for her freedom in those moments. Most of her children were placed with their dads, except one of her sons, Caleb. His dad was incarcerated so he had nowhere to go.

At the time, my sister Tot had just moved to South Carolina with her husband. They had only been there for about a week or two and were staying with in-laws, so they couldn't take their grandson in. His paternal grandmother was already caring for her elderly mother, her disabled aunt and her terminally ill husband, so her hands were full. His other uncles and aunts either had their hands full with their children and had no room or just weren't in a position to take care of him. By this point, Tye and I had already taken in four of Scooby's friends. We had said that the last two were "the last ones," but our hearts wouldn't allow us to ignore someone in need, especially a child. We were ready for a break. We said we weren't going to do it. Besides, TJ had been molded into the perfect kid. We didn't need any distractions as Caleb and TJ were the same age but came from two different background structures. This was where it became a conflict.

Tye and I decided we were walking away from this one. Sadly, it became an issue to where Caleb would either go to the State or to someone outside of family. We were not sure what their motives were. Our spirits wouldn't allow us to rest until we stepped up and took responsibility for him.

The fight within was over. We did the right thing and welcomed him into our home with open arms. It was a struggle with TJ in the beginning. He was happy to have a playmate the same age as him under the same roof. When Caleb would play certain songs, TJ would tell him that they weren't allowed to listen to that kind of music. The same went for anything else that went against our house rules. Eventually, Caleb's behavior started rubbing off on TJ. He started being messy. His mannerism started to change. "Yes, Ma'am" or "Yes, Sir" turned into, "Yeah."

When he cleaned up, instead of putting things away in their respective places, he learned to hide things under his bed, and under drawers. They'd put trash and food inside of drawers, and they would junk up the closet. He started lying and sneaking things. This made my nerves so bad! I started punishing them.

Caleb was used to the punishments. He was a sweet kid. He was mischievous and destructive; no type of punishment had a lasting effect on him. TJ, on the other hand, couldn't stand getting his things taken away. That was new to him, and he wasn't trying to get used to it. He went back to being truthful.

He told Caleb, "You can get in trouble by yourself!"

Homeboy meant that!

Caleb had his struggles with right and wrong, this definitely kept us going. Meanwhile, we adopted a pit bull one weekend in August while Caleb was out visiting his paternal grandmother. One of my husband's clients found a full bred Red Nose puppy wandering down 103rd Street. He attempted to look for the owner but had no luck. He couldn't keep the pup, so we took him in and continued to search. We put him on a few social media posts, checked the humane society and then went to the vet to see if he was chipped. We ended up keeping him. My husband's client named him Chopper, so we kept that name for him. I have always loved and wanted a pit, but when I actually had him in my car, I was a bit nervous. This was our first time meeting. We were in my 2013 Buick Lacrosse. This joker had his nails in my leather seats. Because his teeth were pointing in my direction and his tongue was hanging out, I excused it. I excused the nails in my seat, because he was super cute. He was as friendly as he could be. It took no time for me to fall in love with him. I'm a huge dog lover. As a matter of fact, he already had a playmate waiting for him. Pep. Well, Pep isn't much of a playmate. We had him for seven years, and he was already old when he got him. My husband's friend and co-worker gave him to us when he moved to Miami in 2014. He is set in his ways. You have to catch him on a good day to get him to play.

Well, Caleb came home and was initially afraid of Chopper. He was on his best behavior for a day or two until he got used to him. Then, he was back to his old self again. Chopper was good for Caleb. No matter how much Caleb would bully him around, Chopper would never bite him or act aggressively towards him. We started taking Chopper outside; he became the neighborhood kids' dog. There were three other pit bulls on the street, but everyone wanted to play with Chopper, except one little girl. She was afraid of dogs. Her brother wasn't. He tried to get her to not be afraid. She wasn't having it.

Two of the girls who would come and play were sisters. They had a Blue Nose Pit, but he was mean. They, too, enjoyed coming to my house to play with our dog. They would have him come outside while they jumped on the trampoline, because they knew he would jump on while they were on it. They would also call him then run so he could chase them. He was a puppy living life.

Everything was starting to normalize. I was planning my graduation-birthday trip to Indiana. My plan was to walk across the graduation stage as my long hair draped my graduation cap that read, *The best birthday gift ever*. I pictured my smile lighting up the whole room.

No one would have known the extent of what I overcame, but I envisioned myself having the glow of a victorious woman. My black gown would have my red and black cord and my blue and gold cord hanging around my neck in honor of my achievements. I made it into the Alpha Beta Kappa Honor Society as well as the Society for Collegiate Leadership & Achievement. I'd also have my Alpha Beta Kappa pin affixed to the gown. Those achievements meant a lot to me, because of everything I had to endure and overcome as a student. I'd always wanted to become a member of a sorority but I never attended a school that had an open chapter. I know this wasn't the same thing, but it was a key because of my GPA. I couldn't wait to network with some of the alumni after the commencement, knowing I had earned this!

Mom was planning to come out. She was going to make sure my dad got out to Indiana as well. My sister-friend Arnitra has been with me every step of the way, not just for school and my wedding, but in every aspect of life. She was planning to be there and so was my brother Charles then Covid-19 hit. It shut the whole country down. Traveling plans from all around the world basically came to a halt. Not only was I not going to walk across the stage, neither were the high school graduates of 2020 who never experienced graduation. Grad Nite, prom, all of the things that seniors were looking forward to, they would not experience. I was sad but okay that things fell through, because I had graduated twice before: once in high school and once at Jones College. I didn't actually earn my degree at Jones College. I had Dasjuan and couldn't do my internship and work a full-time job at the same time. I still walked across the stage. I felt sorrow for those who were robbed of those pleasures.

My graduation was pushed back a few months before they decided to have a virtual one, because we couldn't gather within six feet of each other. Plus, there was a mask mandate across the country. The world was changing. While some people went into panic mode, others went into action. People started getting creative with graduation. We started seeing virtual graduations in people's homes while family members attended online. We saw an increase in yard signs of the graduates, and my favorite was graduation parades of vehicles. This was what my husband and mom surprised me with. Mom came by because she wanted to get cap and gown pictures. We first started taking pictures in the living room in my plain clothes. Because we weren't going anywhere, I had on my pink and white flannel shirt, a hot pink tank top, knee-length cut-off denim shorts, my Dr. Seuss "Oh the Places You'll Go" socks, and my pink and white Jordans. I specifically wore those socks for that occasion, because going back to school was definitely outside of my comfort zone. I was too old, had a family of my own, and I wasn't as smart as I used to be. I had all of these reasons for why I shouldn't go back to school until I got fired from Tulsa Welding School. At that point, the only reason I needed was my own sense to feel empowered.

I made sure we took a lot of pictures in my socks as a reminder that the possibilities are endless as long as you have an open mind. After we spent enough time in the house, Mom and Tye had me put on my cap and gown so that we could take photos in my backyard. What I didn't know was they were on a schedule. We went out of my backdoor and started taking pictures on the balcony. The balcony sits on a hillslope that greets a retention pond. There is an oak tree that rests on the corner of my balcony that compliments the view of the pond, so it makes beautiful scenery for the pictures.

As my mom kept me busy posing, my husband and Scooby were in the front getting the cars and cupcakes ready. I kept asking for my husband but Mom came up with some kind of excuse, and I believed her. I remember her telling me that he was coming.

Finally, Mom said, "Let's go and take pictures in the front with your flowers and—"

Boom! Cars lined the street on both sides as they were coming and going, honking as the people were smiling.

I was speechless! I saw people who I haven't seen in a long time! I saw family members, friends, my best friend Kutana, and her family were there. Her mom even came out to support me! I haven't seen her since my early twenties! That blew my mind! My church family was there, and they represented! I had no idea that TJ's godmother, Chenee, was in on it, too. She was coordinating the parade. I knew that come hell and high water Arnitra would be there. That was no surprise, but it sure did feel good to know she was there. Mr. Smith, the man who changed my life in high school, was also there. I hadn't seen him in forever either. Carla, another friend of mine from church, not only came to the parade, but she also took me out to lunch and ice cream to celebrate my birthday/graduation. It was exhilarating to know that I had so many people supporting my journey.

Caleb was straight-faced. I mean, totally emotionless. I couldn't get him to smile in any of my pictures. I wasn't going to let him ruin my joy. I was missing Jabari though. He already had plans on going to Atlanta with his dad to see his aunt, so that's why he wasn't there. We took our own pictures with my cap and gown on over my fireplace with my cell phone the night before the parade. He hugged me tight, congratulated me, and told me how proud he was of me. He left with his dad later that evening. That boy may run my nerves, but he loves his mother. Everyone who knows us, can attest to that.

A few days prior to the graduation parade, Scooby came to me as I was in my room making my bed. He hung around for a bit. I knew something was on his mind, but I was waiting for him to open up. We always talk about everything, so I knew it would eventually come out.

After some small talk he said, "Monique is pregnant."

I burst out in laughter for two reasons. He couldn't understand what was funny. He was still in school and hadn't given up at this time on enlisting into the military. Even though he had messed up with the Air Force when he got arrested, the Navy was still an option.

I looked at him and said, "Son, I don't know why you are walking around here sad-faced when you know what it takes to have a baby. Did you think you could play Russian Roulette without eventually catching the bullet?"

Prior to these conversations, he would come to me and tell me about people his age who were having babies and express his disappointment.

I would tell him, "The only difference between you and them is you haven't got caught yet."

I reminded him of that and said, "Tag, you're it."

I was making light of the situation, because it made no sense to be upset, only for it to turn to joy after the thought had grown on me. That's what I call wasted emotions. Life is too short for that. Not only that but I told him Monique was pregnant even before either of them knew she was. He told me she wasn't when I initially stated that. They had just taken a test about two weeks prior to me telling him, and it was negative.

After I questioned the timing, we realized that when God gave me that feeling of her being pregnant, she was about four weeks. I welcomed the idea of Tye and I being grandparents. I would have rather not become a grandma at the age of forty-three, but it is what it is.

School for the children started back in August. I opted for them to attend school virtually, because I felt the risk of them being back in public school was too great with Covid-19 spreading like wildfire. Luckily, TJ and Caleb attended the same school and were in the same class. This made helping out with homework and assisting with classwork a lot easier on me. Caleb liked it, because he didn't have to get up and go anywhere. TJ hated virtual school. He would rather be in a building with his friends. Jabari hated it as well. He blamed his failure on virtual learning when actually he just wasn't trying. When he tried, he succeeded. It's true that virtual learning is not easy, but I would not allow him to use that as an excuse. He wasn't putting his best foot forward.

It was January 6th, 2021 when I lashed out verbally on Jabari, because I was tired of his excuses. He is such a good kid, and it hurt me deeply to see him not applying himself when he is fully capable. I remember the day so well because a lot was going on at once. For starters, this was the thirteenth day that I was haunted by the memories of my childhood. The first day, I was taking a shower, and out of the blue it popped up in my mind. I cried about this -like really cried- for the first time. Not because of what I went through but because of Who brought me through. I realized that when I thought I was going through that traumatic experience by myself, God was with me the whole time. My life could have been worse, but God kept me together. It's true I acted out, but it never consumed me.

I remember saying that if I ever had the opportunity to glorify God to the masses, I would. Anyway, Jabari messed around and told me virtual school was hard.

Something in me snapped, "Let me tell you what hard is. Hard is being taken advantage of by people half your life and as a child, having to figure out how to get through it. Hard is dealing with the stresses of everyday life while going to school; trying to maintain your grades; being worried about my young black boys who don't always make the best decisions everyday; and raising a child who thinks he is privileged and doesn't want to work for anything. Raising a child who wants everything handed to him while still maintaining a smile on my face. So, I won't worry y'all as y'all are worrying me, that's hard!"

When I was finished with him, he went into the kitchen and started cooking, as that is something he loves to do.

I walked outside to cool down for a bit. When I came back in, he gave me the tightest hug ever and told me I was right. He admitted to not trying and told me he was going to change.

Meanwhile, later that evening, I had just finished eating dinner with my husband. We were watching a movie together when I received a phone call from my nephew, Anthony. We call him BMX, because that is his skill with his bike. When he called me he said he needed to talk to me about something. I thought he wanted to talk to me about Caleb, who is his nephew, too.

Caleb had gone back to his mom on the first of January, and that seemed to be a hot topic. Caleb was doing so well with his behavior and everyone started seeing the positive change. He wasn't perfect, but he had made major changes. Until he heard he was going back to his mom, that is. Then, he regressed. She was missing him and wanted him back, so she came and got him. Although we briefly discussed this, that wasn't the reason for his call. I walked outside to talk so I wouldn't continue to disrupt the movie. Chopper followed me out. I stood by my Buick in my driveway when he told me he had a baby on the way. He was super excited, and I was excited that he was looking forward to becoming a father. He had several close calls, but this one was the real deal.

The next thing I knew, Chopper took off running down the

street. He saw Jabari before I did so he went to greet him. He was coming back from the store. I put BMX on hold while I ran after Chopper. As we walked back, he noticed our neighbor's son getting into his truck. He walked by and sniffed him. I apologized to him. I then grabbed Chopper and put him in the house, because he knew better than to run off from me. I continued my conversation with BMX, and then my phone beeped. It was my neighbor telling me that her son said the next time my dog runs up on him, he was going to shoot him. She proceeded to tell me how he would be within his rights and how he worked for JSO (Jacksonville Sheriff's Office). I could care less who he worked for. This joker had just threatened my dog's life.

Chopper may be a dog, but he was a member of my family. In all honesty, this was the second time my dog went up to a member of his family. The first time, I had just bought an invisible fence. I was outside trying to figure out how to work it when my neighbor and her daughter started screaming when Chopper ran over to them. They had a little girl with them. I called Chopper back, but he didn't listen. So, I got up and ran to get him. He saw a kid and wanted to play! He was a puppy. Nevertheless, it was my negligence for not having him on a leash; so, I apologized for him going into their yard. The daughter yelled at me as if I were a child. I took a quick pause to think about my next move. Then, I walked away without saying a word. I had sympathy for the little toddler who feared Chopper. But as for my neighbor's daughter, who may actually be her daughter-in-law, I had to remember that I am a Christian first. In this Christian walk, sometimes you feel like a pushover. However, it is better to walk away than to respond, because we are responsible for our actions, not the other person's. I didn't mind walking away, because I felt like if we had to take it there verbally then we may as well go all the way. I am a stickler for respect, but I'm too old to be fighting. I have come too far in my Christian walk to regress. What's crazy is that when I don't respond, my mind finds a way to replay the scene over and over. I'll end up having different endings with each replay.

Anyway, the next day my neighbor explained why she is terrified of dogs. She told me her experience with her mom and how she was bitten by a dog. I shared how Scooby was bitten three times as a kid and twice in this neighborhood, but I was still trying to be empathetic to her. We are neighbors. We always look out for each other, and I did not want that to change. She and her husband are really kind people; she had just rubbed me the wrong way when she tried to paint my dog out to be bad. Their house has cameras and their cameras captured my dog chasing the girls as they were playing. She tried to convince me that my dog was bad by insisting he had hawked the girls down as if he was trying to attack them.

I tried to explain what was happening that day and told her that if they feared Chopper, then they wouldn't come by asking for him to come out almost every day.

We are all neighbors, "Ask them if you really want to know," I said.

She was convinced in her own mind that my dog was terrorizing children and that her granddaughter was an example of that. She told me she no longer goes out in the morning to attend to her garden because of Chopper. He wasn't even out in the mornings, but she feared him that much just knowing he was nearby. I stopped letting Chopper go outside with kids without me being present.

So when Chopper walked up to her son that night, I guess, "It makes it right for him to shoot my dog."

It took days and constant prayer for the Lord to remove the thoughts that I had in my head, because it was far from being Christ-like. I had nothing but wrath in my head, but I knew I couldn't carry on like that. I think it was rough for me to move on, because -as I mentioned- I was reliving my trauma for thirteen days. I was dealing with Jabari. And I was hurting for our country for what happened at the Pentagon that day. That was when the rioters stormed the Capitol. I just picked up my boxing gloves and let out all of my aggression on my punching bag.

You never know what someone may be going through, so always be kind. I believe that the lack of kindness is one cause for so much violence in the world. People forget the number one rule: treat others as you would yourself. If we loved our neighbors as we do ourselves then I believe this would solve most of the world's problems today. Everyone doesn't have self-control, and many of those who do, don't practice it. So they react on impulse. I'm glad God loved me enough to redirect me. He put me on a path to peace that at times surpasses all understanding.

This is how I am able to forgive when others say, "They wouldn't be able to," or walk away from certain situations when others may not be able to.

With God anything is possible. I am not perfect. I don't always read my Bible daily like I should. My every thought isn't Christian-like. But what I have learned over time is that, as a Christian, you have two spirits. You have your human spirit, the one you were born with and the Holy Spirit that resides inside of you after you become a born again Christian. This means you now are a child of God, believing and trusting in the name of Jesus. To be clear, we are all creations of God; we aren't all God's children. So, once one has been adopted into the family, the Holy Spirit is God's seal on His people. He will regenerate and renew you as a believer in Christ.

He does so many things, including guarding you from your fleshly desires. But here's the thing, you must continue to feed the spirit. Whatever spirit you feed the most will be the dominant one. If you continue to feed into your fleshly desires and not read God's Word, not pray, and not surround yourself with people who will uplift you rather than tear you down, then that spirit will be more dominant. This is why if I do nothing else, I pray daily, several times a day.

For a long time, I was ashamed of my past. I knew better but I hadn't always done better when it came to things I had done in my life. But then I realized that God did not allow me to go through things just to be ashamed, to walk through life as if it didn't exist. God brought me through to be a testimony to his power, his greatness, and his agape love. This is why I dedicate each day to Him by dying to myself daily. Because of God's love for me, I practice not giving into my fleshly desires.

My past doesn't define me, but it is a definitive testimony of God's power. For a while, my bones were dry because of what I went through. I had convinced myself that I wasn't smart enough or good enough or talented enough to do certain tasks that were set before me. Insecurities had set in. I didn't realize it at the time, but it showed in my actions. God brought me out of my negative thinking. He evicted those unhealthy thoughts and replaced them with His goodness. He gave me peace that surpasses all understanding!

www.ingramcontent.com/pod-product-compliance
Lightning Source LLC
Chambersburg PA
CBHW070415120526
44590CB00014B/1403